Children and Learning Difficulties

Children and Learning Difficulties

Onita Nakra

ALLIED PUBLISHERS PVT. LTD.

New Delhi • Mumbai • Kolkata • Chennai • Bangalore • Hyderabad

ALLIED PUBLISHERS PRIVATE LIMITED

D-5, Sector-2, **Noida**–201 301
Ph. Nos.: 0120-4320295/2542557/4352866
E-mail: delhi.books@alliedpublishers.com

17 Chittaranjan Avenue, **Kolkata**–700072
Ph.: 033-22129618 • E-mail: cal.books@alliedpublishers.com

15 J.N. Heredia Marg, Ballard Estate, **Mumbai**–400001
Ph.: 022-42126969 • E-mail: mumbai.books@alliedpublishers.com

No. 25/10, Commander-in-Chief Road, Ethiraj Lane (Next to Post Office)
Egmore, **Chennai**–600008
Ph.: 044-28223938 • E-mail: chennai.books@alliedpublishers.com

P.B. No. 9932, No. 15, 3rd Floor (Next to Vijaya Bank), 5th Cross, Gandhinagar,
Karnataka, **Bangalore**–560009. Ph.: 080-41530285 / 22386239
• E-mail: bngl.journals@alliedpublishers.com / apsabng@airtelmail.in

Sri Jayalakshmi Nilayam, No. 3-4-510, 3rd Floor (Above More Super Market)
Barkatpura, **Hyderabad**–500027
Ph.: 040-27551811, 040-27551812 • E-mail: hyd.books@alliedpublishers.com

Website: www.alliedpublishers.com

First Edition, 1996
Second Edition, 2007
Third Edition, 2017
Fourth Thoroughly Revised Edition, 2023

ISBN: 978-93-90951-54-3

Published by Sunil Sachdev and printed by Ravi Sachdev
at Allied Publishers Pvt. Ltd., D-5, Sector-2, Noida–201 301

This book is

dedicated

to

Sri Sathya Sai Baba and MN

Preface

This book reflects the changing face of learning disability and the new educational directions emerging from recent research. The last decade has seen several new developments in every aspect of learning disability from definition to intervention. In India, there has been a quantum jump in awareness about the disability. Teachers and parents are far more comfortable now about using terms such as *dyslexia, spelling disorder, writing disorders* than they were earlier. Complementing this is a growing familiarity and understanding of students' educational needs. Schools are open to discussions about what they can do to help the child with a learning disability. The focus has shifted to improving teaching practices rather than just condemning the child with a label that often can become stigmatising.

The compelling reason for a new, revised edition of the book is to ensure that readers are receiving the most current information about learning disabilities. At it's simplest level, the term "learning disability" continues to mean difficulties in reading, writing or mathematics. Recent research from brain imaging studies however indicates that we can now identify, with medical precision, which areas of language are affected. Brain research has undoubtedly impacted how we view learning disabilities, especially in the area of reading.

The book is designed to guide teachers and parents through the many mazes of learning disabilities. *Section One* focuses on new trends in the field, and how the changing definition of learning disability impacts learning in the classroom. *Section Two* takes the reader into the depths of each of the affected areas – reading, writing, language, and mathematics. Of special interest is the expanded chapter on the learning disabled adolescent and adult. Many of the youngsters with learning disability are now in college and in mainstreamed professions. Their experiences carry valuable lessons for teachers and educators. The field of adult learning disability is still in its infancy in India but there is a lot happening in other countries, which we can adapt. *Section Three* focuses on the assessment process and discusses some key principles for designing intervention programs.

The *Appendices* include resources that teachers and parents should find very helpful. Wherever possible, an attempt has been made to offer well-researched websites and links to authentic sources. A special thanks to the many learning disabled students whose stories have touched our lives in different ways. And last but not least, I'd like to express my gratitude to my husband Manoj Nakra whose faith in me has inspired me in every pursuit.

Contents

Section–I
An Introduction to Learning Disability

Section–III
Assessment and Remediation

Appendices

SECTION-I

An Introduction to Learning Disability

CHAPTER 1

Understanding Learning Disability

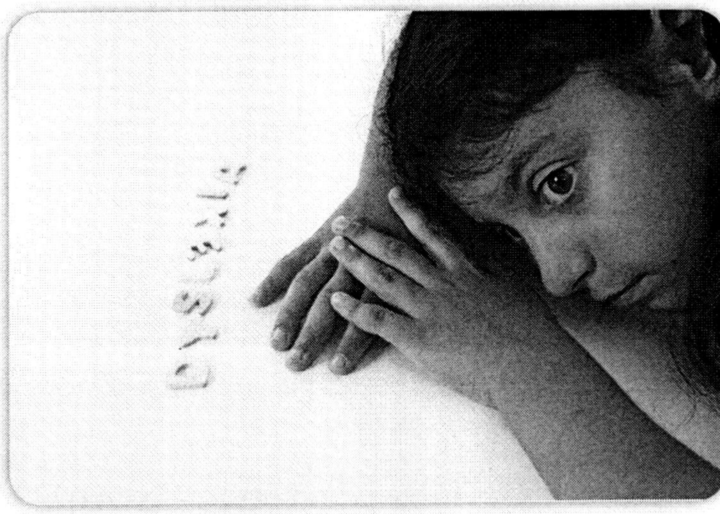

Defining Learning Disability

The term *learning disability* is used to describe a specific population of children, adolescents and adults who have problems in learning. These problems are generally in the areas of reading, writing, spellings, and mathematics. Parents and teachers usually discover the problem when the child begins to struggle with schoolwork. Teachers may notice a great difference between a student's oral performance, which could be very good, and his written work. Surprisingly, there is a great deal of individual variation among children with a learning disability. Parents provide different versions of the disability:

"My ten-year old daughter Priya hates to read. She reads very slowly, often misses letters, and cannot pronounce simple words."

"Deepak cannot copy from the blackboard. His handwriting is illegible and the teacher is always complaining about his poor spellings. He forgets names of places, cannot identify characters in a story and has a limited vocabulary."

"Aditya speaks very well but cannot even write a sentence."

There could be comments in the child's school notebooks to say, "She needs to work harder;" or, "His spellings are very weak," testifying to the rather complex nature of a learning disability. The terminology itself can be quite daunting and upsetting for parents. "Why do you call my son *disabled* when there is nothing physically or mentally wrong with him?" is quite a common parental reaction.

A learning disability is found across all ages and socio-economic classes. It is *not* a type of mental retardation as sometimes mistakenly thought, in fact, IQ scores could fall in the very high range. However, a learning disability can occur along with other handicapping conditions, for example with sensory impairment, emotional and behavioural disorders, and mental retardation. In such cases it is considered a secondary and not the primary handicap.

Defining Learning Disability—An Historical Overview

In the early 1960's, the difficulty that many children were having with learning began to attract serious attention in the United States. An increasing number of children demonstrating difficulties in reading, writing and mathematics were identified as falling behind grade level work. These children were otherwise bright, fairly articulate in their verbal expression, and did not appear to have any form of mental retardation, sensory handicap or visual impairment. Educators and professionals began to take these learning difficulties seriously. On April 6, 1963, Dr. Samuel Kirk addressed a gathering of anxious parents in Chicago, at which he first used the term *learning disability* to describe these children (Hallahan and Cruickshank, 1973, p. 4):

> ...this meeting is not concerned with children who have sensory handicaps, such as the deaf or the blind, or with children who are mentally retarded... It is concerned primarily with children who can see and hear and who do not have marked intellectual deficits, but who show deviations in behavior and in psychological

> development to such an extent that they are unable to adjust in the home or to learn by ordinary methods in school.

The term *"learning disability"* was formally accepted and an organization called the Association for Children with Learning Disabilities (ACLD) was started to provide services for individuals of all ages.

Soon after this meeting, there was a flood of terms and medical phrases to describe the condition, terms such as brain damage, organic disorders, aphasia, minimal brain damage, perceptual handicaps and so on. Professionals could not reach any agreement on terminology, though many parents resented the use of medical terms such as brain damage. In 1967, Johnson and Myklebust suggested that neurological disturbances could be responsible for learning disabilities and suggested the term psychoneurological learning disability. While the controversy continued unabated, the National Advisory Committee on Handicapped Children passed an Act in 1969, which defined learning problems in this way:

> Children with special learning disabilities exhibit a disorder in one or more of the basic psychological processes involved in understanding or in using spoken or written language. These may be manifested in disorders of listening, thinking, talking, reading, writing, spelling, or arithmetic. They include conditions that have been referred to as perceptual handicaps, brain injury, minimal brain dysfunction, dyslexia, developmental aphasia, etc. They do not include learning problems that are due primarily to visual, hearing, or motor handicaps, to mental retardation, emotional disturbance, or to environmental disadvantage.

The 1969 Act passed in the United States of America allowed learning disabled children to receive federal funding and grants for special services in American schools. By 1976, 260,000 children were receiving services (National Advisory Committee on the Handicapped, 1976, p. 2). But one alarming offshoot was that the number of children being labeled "learning disabled" increased. It appeared that since no specific criteria had been laid down to decide which students were truly learning disabled, teachers were using this category as a dumping ground for low achievers and for any student who failed to learn! So in 1976, it was proposed that some additional specific criteria were needed to clearly separate the learning disabled from other slow learners.

The Federal Definition

In 1977, the U.S. Office of Education brought out a definition of learning disability, which has continued to dominate education for well over two decades. It said:

> "Specific learning disability means a disorder in one or more of the basic psychological processes involved in understanding or in using language, spoken or written, which may manifest itself in an imperfect ability to listen, think, speak, read, write, spell, or to do mathematical calculations. The term includes such conditions as perceptual handicaps, brain injury, minimal brain dysfunction, dyslexia, and developmental aphasia. The term does not include children who have learning problems, which are primarily the result of visual, hearing, or motor handicaps, of mental retardation, of emotional disturbance, or of environmental, cultural, or economic disadvantage." (Federal Register, 1977, p. 65083).

The NJCLD Definition

In 1997, the National Joint Committee for Learning Disabilities (NJCLD, USA) issued an alternative definition:

> Learning disabilities is a general term that refers to a heterogeneous group of disorders manifested by significant difficulties in the acquisition and use of listening, speaking, reading, writing, reasoning, or mathematical abilities. These disorders are intrinsic to the individual, presumed to be due to central nervous dysfunction, and may occur across the life span.

It was clarified that problems in self-regulatory behaviours, social perception and social interaction may exist with learning difficulties, but do not by themselves constitute a learning disability. The NJCLD definition has several advantages over the Federal definition. It acknowledges that the disability may occur at any age. It deletes the phrase *basic psychological processes* and replaces it with the statement that the problem is "intrinsic" to the person and may "be due to central nervous system dysfunction." It rejects ill-defined conditions (perceptual handicaps, minimal brain dysfunction) that caused a great deal of confusion in the past. It clarifies that a learning disability can occur with other handicaps, and diagnosis must determine if it is a primary or secondary condition.

IDEA's Definition of "Learning Disability"

More recently, the American Special Education law, the Individuals with Disabilities Education Act (IDEA, 2002) defines a specific learning disability as:

> "...a disorder in one or more of the basic psychological processes involved in understanding or in using language, spoken or written, that may manifest itself in an imperfect ability to listen, think, speak, read, write, spell, or do mathematical calculations, including conditions such as perceptual disabilities, brain injury, minimal brain dysfunction, dyslexia, and developmental aphasia. However, learning disabilities do not include learning problems that are primarily the result of visual, hearing, or motor disabilities, of mental retardation, of emotional disturbance, or of environmental, cultural, or economic disadvantage." 34 Code of Federal Regulations §300.7(c)(10)

For the purposes of consistency, the IDEA definition of a learning disability will be adhered to in this book. It appears to be a comprehensive definition; it is all-inclusive without being discriminatory. More important, the definition lends itself to operational behaviours in the classroom.

This brief, historical review highlights the complex nature of learning disability. (A more detailed analysis can be found in an article by K. Kavale and S.R. Fornress entitled *What definitions of LD say and don't say: A critical analysis.* Journal of Learning Disabilities, 2000, May–June, 33(3), pp. 239–56).

More importantly, the review suggests that there are two significant aspects latent in the definitions.

1. **The learning disabled individual must show a discrepancy between achievement and intelligence.** A discrepancy is any difference between two findings. For example, the teacher might say, "Deepa speaks well in class but cannot write sentences." Or, using an IQ test, we may find that though Deepa is doing poorly in reading and spelling, her innate ability scores are average or above average. Relative to her ability, she is underachieving. She would also probably be doing poorly compared to her classmates. The discrepancy model of identifying learning disability is fraught with controversies. Much of the confusion stems from there not being any clear guidelines about what really signifies a significant discrepancy. Will an IQ test (which has so many items that require the child to read or process visual/verbal information) accurately reflect the child's innate aptitude?

Let's look at how discrepancies work. Most educational and psychological tests of intelligence (or aptitude) have an average score of 100. This is referred to as a standard score because all of the raw scores earned on the tests are put in a standard model that results in a bell curve. In the bell curve most individuals achieve around the average score. In fact 68% of children who take achievement and intelligence tests will have a score within a range from 85–115. Thus if a child's intelligence is 110, his reading score too should be very close to that score. But if he obtains a standard score of 90 on a standardized reading test, we can assume he is achieving 20 points below his predicted reading score. There is a difference of 20 points between his ability and current achievement, which indicates the possibility of a learning disability. This is a difference greater than one standard deviation (SD) which is considered a *statistically significant* discrepancy.

On IQ tests (such as the WISC), discrepancies between Index scores help to identify a learning disability. For example, low scores on the

Processing Speed Index or the Working Memory Index could indicate a possible learning disability.

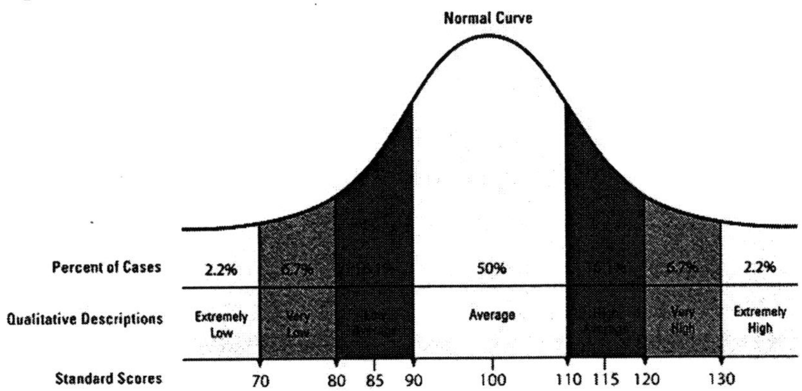

Figure 1: The Bell Curve

Despite the controversy that surrounds the use of the discrepancy criteria, it continues to be the single most used criteria for diagnosing and placing learning disabled children in special programs, and is mandatory in many states in the USA. Experts have argued against this method of analysis (Kavale, 1995, Anastasi and Urbina, 1997), describing it as a misuse of results. They warn that the discrepancy score alone should never be used as the sole criterion for identification, and should be viewed as just one piece of the puzzle. Unfortunately, until we have access to a more scientific methodology, it seems that the discrepancy model is here to stay.

2. **Handicaps such as mental retardation, visual and hearing impairment and emotional/behavioural disorders must be ruled out.** Most definitions insist that when identifying a learning disabled person, the presence of other handicaps must be excluded. A learning disability could occur in the presence of factors such as a low socio-economic environment, inadequate exposure to language, or lack of educational opportunities. It may also occur concomitantly with other handicapping conditions such as sensory impairment, mental retardation, or serious emotional disturbance. But in these cases the learning disability should be considered a *secondary* condition. It is

always helpful to remember that a primary learning disability does not include organic, sensory-type impairments.

Learning Disability in India: Is There Any Law?

In India, the Persons With Disabilities Act (PWD, 1995) has been landmark legislation for the disabled in general. Unfortunately, *learning disability* is not mentioned anywhere in this Act. There was a law case brought against the Delhi University in 2004 to highlight this fact. Shikhar Narang, a student with dyslexia, was denied the benefit of 3% reservation meant for disabled students. The Disabled Rights Group filed a case and in 2004, the Delhi High Court passed a landmark interim order stating that students with dyslexia be given admission under the disability quota. Though the field of learning disability in India fails to get much support from Government agencies, a lot of excellent support is provided by non-government organizations (NGOs). Many private schools try to individualize and modify the curriculum to meet the needs of the dyslexic student. Teachers' awareness of the nature of the problem has grown hugely over the past ten years though research is still in its infancy. Most of the research findings come to us from the United States or UK. Studies on reading and writing may not be the best fit for a country where English is not the first language. However, due to the paucity of research in India, we have to draw upon the knowledge base provided by more developed countries. Fortunately, principles of good teaching and best practices in reading and mathematics are universal, and these do not require any law—only a commitment to ensure that the students receive a fair deal in any school system where they may be studying.

Some Issues and Concerns

Different Types of Learning Disability

There are many different types of learning disability and there is a great deal of variation within individuals. A learning disabled child can be excellent in mathematics and yet do very poorly in reading and writing. Another may find it very difficult to write but have good verbal skills. There may be a great deal of variation within subject areas. For example, both Deepak and Adil perform poorly in written language. However Deepak's problem is that he cannot express his thoughts in writing whereas Adil cannot make the basic association between sound and symbol. A learning disability can be confined to academic performance in subjects such as reading, writing or arithmetic, or impact the child's performance in other areas such as art, athletics, listening, attention and so on. Each learning disabled individual has a unique set of characteristics, which must be recognized for effective educational intervention to occur.

The Importance of Early Intervention

A learning disability is usually diagnosed when a child enters primary school. The difficulty could be exaggerated in the higher classes when the focus of instruction is less on basic skills and more on content information. A child entering grade 4 or 5 is expected to read fluently, copy notes from the board, write essays, and answer questions on a given passage. A fair amount of abstract reasoning is demanded and a massive burden placed on memory. This is why early diagnosis is very important. Approaches used in grade one cannot be used when the child is older and it is time consuming to teach a child in middle school basic reading skills using phonics or sentence cards. The academic lag continues to increase with time, and if no assistance is provided, there is the risk of the child not completing school. Dropout rates for the learning disabled is fairly high.

Unfortunately parents take a long time to acknowledge there could be something wrong with their child. Ignorance about the disability is prevalent and does a lot of harm by delaying intervention. Teachers too have a major role to play in helping to detect a learning disability, but often they may not know what signs and behaviours to look for. Usually, a teacher's typical response is to say that the child is "very lazy," "is not trying hard enough," or that parents "must take more interest in his homework." Sometimes if a child is lucky he will find a teacher who realizes that the child is neither lazy nor a shirker but that "there is something wrong" in the way he is processing information.

Guided by her intuition and "gut feel" a sensitive teacher can force parents to seek expert help for the child, thus saving valuable time. Unfortunately when she conveys her doubts to the parents they may be reluctant to accept her assessment. Part of this reluctance is owing to their fear that the school authorities may ask them to remove their child from the school. Parental fears are not totally misplaced. Few schools are equipped with specialized resources and may be unable to offer appropriate services to the child. Although teachers help in diagnosing the problem, they are seldom trained to implement any kind of remedial teaching in the classroom. There are constraints of time, large class sizes, and excessive syllabus to be completed. In addition, teachers tend to be inflexible about changing their own methods of teaching and evaluation. For example, instead of expecting the child to complete five essay questions in a three-hour period, it would be more realistic to allow the child extra time for writing and examine him orally on part of the examination. Schools must permit the students to use some alternative tools of learning, for example, a computer or a calculator if necessary. Early diagnosis needs to be supported by a positive attitude from the schools otherwise it merely serves to deny the child an appropriate education.

The Learning Disabled Adult

Very little attention is paid to the needs of the learning disabled person at the secondary and post secondary levels. In India, no specific services are offered to students entering the University, although in other parts of the world, colleges develop programs explicitly to meet the needs of learning disabled adults.[1]

Prevalence of Learning Disability

The actual number of children who have a learning disability in India is difficult to obtain because no national census has been taken. According to the National Council of Educational Research and Training (NCERT) in New Delhi, there has been no systematic collection of data and they follow the figures generally quoted by

[1] See Chapter 8.

international agencies. Figures issued by American educators place the number at 10–12 percent.

Identifying Bilingual Students with a Learning Disability

The relationship between learning disability and students who are non-native speakers of English needs to be further explored. It can be quite confusing for teachers and parents to determine if a student is struggling because he does not speak English at home or because he has a true learning disability period. Unfortunately there is very little research on this subject, and even less on learning disability in Hindi or other native languages. Students who do not receive English language inputs at home may exhibit lower academic achievement, particularly in reading and writing and it's possible they are wrongly labelled as having a learning disability. Intelligence tests particularly tend to underestimate the ability of non-native English speakers, since they are conducted in English and biased in favour of native English speakers.

Nag-Arulmani, Reddy, and Buckley (2003) conducted a study in India looking at 118, 7–9 year olds. 90 of these students had reading difficulties in English and 28 were without reading difficulties. All students had been studying English since Grade 1, reported use of at least two languages at home, including Kannada. The researchers randomly assigned them to three groups—a phonological intervention group, a control group, and a language exposure intervention group. They found that the group that received explicit phonological intervention showed significantly higher gains in reading than the other two groups. The study affirmed that early intervention programs that combine phonological awareness with other strategies used with ESL (English as a second language) students yield the most benefits.

Another finding from the review of literature (Klingner *et al.*, 2006) is that it is important to include second language experts when evaluating bilingual students for a possible learning disability.

Clearly, then, there is a great need to conduct more research with students who have a learning disability and belong to non-English speaking backgrounds.

References

Anastasi, A. & Urbina, S. (1997). *Psychological testing.* Englewood Cliffs, N.J.: Prentice-Hall.

Hallahan, D. & Cruickshank, W. (1973). *Psychoeducational Foundation of Learning Disabilities.* Englewood Cliffs, N.J.: Prentice-Hall, Inc.

Johnson, D.J. & Myklebust, H.R. (1967). *Learning Disabilities: Educational Principles and Practices.* New York: Grune and Stratton.

Kavale, K.A. (1995). Setting the record straight on learning disabilities and low achievement: The tortuous path of ideology. *Learning Disabilities Research & Practice, 10,* 145–152.

Kavale, K.A. & Forness, S.R. (2000). What definitions of learning disability say and don't say: A critical analysis. *Journal of Learning Disabilities, 33,* 239–256.

Klingner, J.K., Articles, A.J. & Barletta, L.M. In *English language learners who struggle with Reading: Language acquisition or LD? Journal of Learning Disabilities,* Vol. 39, Number 2, March/April 2006, pp. 108–128.

Nag-Arulmani, S., Reddy, V. & Buckley, S. (2003). *Journal of Research in Reading, 26,* 49–68.

National Joint Committee for Learning Disabilities: Issues on definition. Tampa, Florida, 1981.

CHAPTER 2

Characteristics of Learning Disabilities

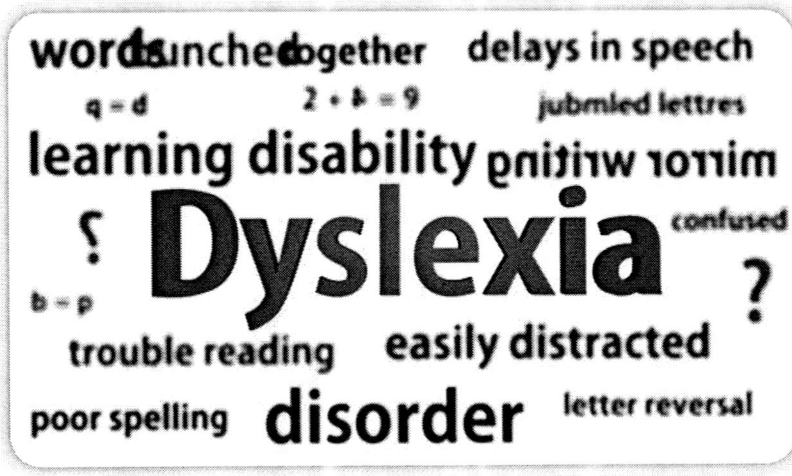

Introduction

A question frequently asked by parents and educators is: "What are the signs and symptoms that help us to recognize whether a child is learning disabled? Are there any typical signs or behaviours that determine a learning disability?" All underachieving students are not learning disabled. In addition, there is so much of individual variation within the learning disabled group that it is not always possible to specify clear-cut characteristics. The literature cites as many as fifteen characteristics, many of which are redundant. However, based on the frequency of occurrence, the following characteristics have been identified as widely prevalent in individuals with learning disability:

1. Disorders of attention.
2. Perceptual impairments.
3. General coordination deficits.
4. Disorders of memory and thinking.

5. Specific difficulties in the areas of reading, arithmetic, writing and spelling.
6. Disorders of speech and hearing.

The next section discusses some of the most important and well researched of these characteristics.

1. *Disorders of Attention*

Attention is the ability to concentrate on a task long enough to grasp its essential features. Learning-disabled individuals are frequently described as having a short attention span and lacking in concentration, but this does not mean that all inattentive children are learning disabled. A child may have an attention disorder for many reasons. He may have an undetected hearing loss or poor eyesight so that he tunes out when the teacher is teaching. Depression, anxiety, emotional problems or stress can lead to problems of concentration. Studies confirm that learning disabled persons are considerably inferior in selective attention (they cannot select the relevant details), and that they cannot maintain attention till the task is completed.

A significant characteristic frequently associated with learning disability is **hyperactivity**, although the relationship between the two is still not clearly substantiated. Psychiatrists refer to hyperactivity as an "**attention-deficit hyperactivity disorder**" (ADHD). Hyperactivity is a much-misunderstood term and widely misused. Generally speaking, when teachers describe a student as being "inattentive" or "hyperactive," the term is being loosely applied to almost any off-task behaviour. When teachers have been asked to explain what they understand by the term "hyperactive," they vaguely indicate "he cannot sit in one place," "he is always talking when I am writing on the board," "he is impulsive and answers without thinking." However, for a child to be truly classified as having an attention deficit (with or without hyperactivity), he must exhibit at least six of the specified behaviours, more often than children of the same age. The symptoms (see Table 2.1) should be present for at least six months, and start prior to 7 years of age. Moreover, the behaviour should be consistently exhibited in different settings (at home and in school). Other disorders (such as Mood Disorder, Anxiety Disorder, Disassociative Disorder, or a Personality Disorder) should be excluded.

Table 2.1:(a) DSM-IV-R Criteria for ADHD

Attention Deficit with Inattention
1. Often fails to give close attention to details or makes careless mistakes in schoolwork, work, or other activities
2. Often has difficulty sustaining attention in tasks or play activities
3. Often does not seem to listen when spoken to directly
4. Often does not follow through on instructions and fails to finish schoolwork, chores, or duties in the workplace (not due to oppositional behaviour or failure to understand instructions)
5. Often has difficulty organizing tasks and activities
6. Often avoids, dislikes, or is reluctant to engage in tasks that require sustained mental effort (such as schoolwork or homework)
7. Often loses things necessary for tasks or activities (e.g., toys, school assignments, pencils, books, or tools)
8. Is often easily distracted by extraneous stimuli
9. Is often forgetful in daily activities

Table 2.1(b): DSM-IV-R Criteria for ADHD

Attention Deficit with Hyperactivity
1. Often fidgets with hands or feet or squirms in seat
2. Often leaves seat in classroom or in other situations in which remaining seated is expected
3. Often runs about or climbs excessively in situations in which it is inappropriate (in adolescents or adults, may be limited to subjective feelings of restlessness)
4. Often has difficulty playing or engaging in leisure activities quietly
5. Is often "on the go" or often acts as if "driven by a motor"
6. Often talks excessively
Attention Deficit with Impulsivity
1. Often blurts out answers before questions have been completed
2. Often has difficulty awaiting turn
3. Often interrupts or intrudes on others (e.g., butts into conversations or games)

The American Psychiatric Association specifies three different kinds of attention deficits:

1. Attention deficits with inattention (ADD)
2. Attention deficit with hyperactivity (ADHD)
3. Attention deficit with impulsivity

A psychologist or psychiatrist should make the diagnosis of attention deficits. Behaviour rating forms (such as the Conner's Rating Scale) are used to collect information from parents and teachers. Observations in class are very useful in determining to what extent the attention deficit is interfering with the child's learning. A child who is unable to read fluently, or cannot understand the content material, will display more inattentive behaviours. This is why children with difficulties in reading, writing and arithmetic are frequently described as "inattentive" or "hyperactive." However, they may not be hyperactive in the true clinical sense of the word.

Stimulant drugs are generally used for students with hyperactive behaviour and attention deficits. Drugs such as Ritalin, Dexedrine, and Cylert are most widely used and must be taken under a physician's care. Some negative side effects reported are lethargy, poor appetite, headache, stomachache, and difficulty falling asleep. Side effects are related to dosage so it is important to start medication under advise of a doctor. Medication can be discontinued during school vacations and weekends to reduce side effects. Children with ADHD do not become addicted to the drug. About 60–80% of school age children with ADHD respond favourably to stimulants. Studies have shown that they decrease impulsiveness and improve attention span, gross and fine motor coordination, handwriting, and general compliance. However, in order to establish a more permanent, long lasting change medication needs to be combined with other approaches such as behaviour modification, cognitive strategies, and self-monitoring strategies.

2. *Disorders of Memory*

Persons with a learning disability are generally characterized by inefficient memory systems. This means that they are unable to spontaneously use rehearsal strategies, or reorganize information in a meaningful way. Early research suggested this occurred because they could not retrieve stored information efficiently. More recent theories focus on their inability to impose structure on information, which is a key factor in memory. It is still not clear whether memory disorders are due to inefficient rehearsal strategies, poor cognitive development, or biochemical differences. While it is difficult to pinpoint exactly where the breakdown is occurring, the following characteristics are often present:

1. Difficulty recalling visual material (patterns, spellings, word order in a sentence etc.)
2. Poor performance on tasks requiring auditory discrimination, or aural discrimination.
3. Difficulty using strategies for verbal rehearsal.

3. *Academic Characteristics*

There is little doubt that in the area of academic learning, children with a learning disability are low achievers. They may have problems in the specific areas of reading, writing and mathematics, although it is not necessary that a child poor in spellings will also be poor in mathematics. Difficulties related to schoolwork generally appear as early as kindergarten and continue into adolescence and adulthood. Here is a brief summary of typical learning difficulties. Section 2 provides a detailed discussion of each academic area.

(a) *Disorders of Reading (Dyslexia)*

Dyslexia refers to a specific difficulty in reading but is widely used as an umbrella term to describe all kinds of learning disability. A dyslexic child reads slowly, often reversing letters, words or numbers. The child may try to guess while reading, omitting or adding words not in the text. He may have a poor vocabulary, and weak comprehension. Research has documented that the dyslexic reader fails to perceive and analyse distinctive features automatically; overlooks the sequential features of a story, which affects comprehension; and focuses less on meaning.

(b) *Disorders of Writing (Dysgraphia)*

The area of written language may also be affected. A child may have difficulty forming the letters and/or the speed of writing will be slow. The overall quality of his handwriting could be extremely untidy, perhaps even illegible. The student may have difficulty copying from the board or from his notebooks. Words are frequently omitted and little attention is paid to punctuation or spellings. The total number of words and length of sentences is reduced. The child will have difficulty putting his thoughts down on paper, and demonstrate a reluctance to write.

(c) *Disorders of Mathematical Learning (Dyscalculia)*

Very little research has been done in the area of mathematical disorders and most of the research available focuses on the younger elementary-level student. Many learning-disabled students have problems in the area of numbers. In the primary classes, they may be unable to associate numbers with quantity. They may display a tendency to reverse numbers (write 12 for 21), and confuse *before* and *after*. Spatial orientation and ability to make estimations of space, size, time, shape and weight tends to be poor. Learning-disabled students tend to work on a concrete level and are slow to acquire abstract reasoning skills, which are very necessary for problem solving in the higher classes.

4. *Disorders of Listening*

Listening is a complex process that requires good attention, discrimination and memory systems. Some learning-disabled individuals may find it difficult to make sense of what is said to them. They may struggle to follow directions, or explain the sequence of events in stories and conversations. Other difficulties may include:

1. An inability to recognize words having multiple meanings or words used in different contexts.
2. Difficulty understanding figurative language, idioms, words with multiple meanings
3. Difficulty understanding sarcasm, humour, and play on words.

5. *Disorders of Language*

The relationship between spoken language and learning disability is complex. Studies have found the speech of some learning disabled children to be very limited in structure and content. The child may use a lot of "fillers" such as "uh...uh," "I mean" or may have articulation difficulties. Learning disabled individuals could make grammatical errors while talking and use words incorrectly. Some struggle to express their thoughts and have difficulty retrieving words during conversations.

6. *Perceptual Impairments*

Perception is the cognitive ability to receive and make sense of incoming stimuli. Traditionally, learning-disabled persons were considered to be deficient in perceptual skills, and programs for improving perceptual skills constituted a large part of the intervention process. Over the years, results have shown that this kind of training has almost no benefit for academic achievement. However, since learning disability continues to be associated with poor perceptual ability, perceptual impairments are discussed at some length here.

Visual Perceptual Deficits

The area of visual perception extends over several different fields such as philosophy, physiology, physics and education, making it difficult to agree on a common definition. Educators generally describe visual perception as the process by which visual stimuli is made meaningful to the observer. Visual perception involves a set of sub skills, briefly described below:

(a) Figure-Ground Discrimination: This is the ability to concentrate on what is relevant, and ignore what is irrelevant. For example, when looking at a picture, a child should be able to attend to salient features and not get confused. Children with a learning disability are frequently unable to discriminate between visual details. Or, when reading, they skip lines and have difficulty 'tracking.' They may struggle with other tasks such as labelling diagrams, locating places on a map etc.

(b) **Spatial Relationships:** Spatial relationships are the building blocks of all learning. Concepts related to directionality (such as left/right, under/above), are integral to most tasks, for example, copying a pattern, writing words in a sentence, or solving addition and subtraction sums. Children with a learning disability may experience difficulty in directionality, which could further impact their academic skills.

(c) **Visual Discrimination:** Visual discrimination is the ability to see fine discriminations between objects, letters, numbers and so on. Several theorists hold that learning disabled children are unable to distinguish between letters which look the same such as *b* and *d*; *p* and *q*. Visual discrimination aids fluency in reading and a deficit in this area could aggravate reading difficulties.

(d) **Visual-Motor Integration:** It was Newell Kephart (1977) who introduced programs based on the relationship between perception and physical movement. According to Kephart, perceptual and motor learning go side by side. For example, when a child traces a line, he alters the movement and direction of his hand in response to feedback from visual information. He believed that basic skills—eye-hand coordination, temporal-spatial integration, and form perception—must be taught in their natural order of development. Children who are weak in this area will demonstrate difficulty in buttoning, lacing, cutting, pasting, writing and copying from the board. The shape, size, and position of objects will also confuse them. According to Kephart, children must be taught *motor patterns* and not splinter (isolated) skills, and his training program emphasizes exercises to bring about this "perceptual motor match."

Auditory Perceptual Deficits

Definitions of auditory perception differ from writer to writer. Myklebust (1954) defined it as the ability to select sounds from the environment. Lerner (1976) described it as the process by which sensory data received by the ear is organized. Still others have equated it with central processing of auditory stimuli. However, it is important to remember that auditory perception is different from physiological hearing or auditory acuity. A child may have nothing wrong with his hearing but still be unable to interpret what is heard. The following sub skills offer a comprehensive overview of what the literature describes as auditory perception.

(a) Auditory Discrimination: Auditory discrimination is the ability to hear similarities and differences between two or more sounds. It is a fundamental building block for the phonetic aspects of reading and is discussed at length in Chapter 5. Most tests for reading include a section on auditory discrimination and this requires the child to discriminate between two or more sounds.

(b) Auditory Blending: Auditory blending is a skill specially required for reading. It is the ability to blend or combine sounds to form words. Many dyslexic readers tend to read in a disjointed manner and have difficulty breaking apart and putting together blends *(bl, sp, gr)* and digraphs *(ch, gh, th)*.

(c) Auditory Memory: This is the ability to recall sounds and make sense of what is heard. Some children with a learning disability have a poor memory for sounds and particularly struggle with tasks where they are expected to sequence sounds in the right order (spelling, recall of digits etc.).

7. *Motor Coordination Deficits*

Motor skills include gross motor skills, fine motor skills, balance, laterality, directionality and body image.

(a) **Gross motor skills** include activities such as walking, jumping, catching and so on. Teachers have observed that many children with a learning disability are clumsy and awkward on the playground, unable to perform apparently simple physical exercises such as toe touching. They also find it difficult to perform balancing activities on the beam, or standing on one leg. An interesting research finding reported by Kaluger and Kolson (1978) is that there is an improvement in the listening and comprehension ability of learning disabled children when they are standing (rather than sitting).

(b) **Fine motor skills** are a basic prerequisite for any kind of academic learning. They include activities involving eye and hand movements such as tracing, needlework, bead stringing, lacing, colouring or writing. Learned disabled children sometimes have deficits in fine motor skills, which impacts their handwriting and drawing skills.

(c) **Laterality** Kephart (1977) distinguished laterality from directionality by observing that laterality is complete, internalised motor awareness of the two sides of one's body. We can follow directions only when we know that external objects are situated to the right, left, front, back, above, or behind only in relation to our body. Children with deficits in this area will have difficulty in following commands and instructions such as "sit on the chair on the right side," "take one step forward," or "underline the word."

Haptic Perception

Haptic perception is the process by which information is acquired through the tactile (sense of touch) and kinaesthetic (movement) systems. A child explores the world around him by touching and manipulating objects and absorbing information pertaining to texture, pain, temperature, pressure, and geometric features. However, some learning disabled children may be unable to derive meaning from touching. For example, the quality of "roundness" in a circle, and concepts related to hard/soft, rough/smooth or hot/warm, may not be acquired easily. They may also have problems with kinaesthesia, which includes bodily movements, coordination, body image, directions, and spatial orientation. A child may be unable to write because he doesn't know how to move his hand and cannot produce the up/down strokes required for writing.

Social and Interpersonal Characteristics

For a long time, researchers focussed primarily on academic and cognitive characteristics of learning disabled persons but more recently there has been an increasing interest in social and emotional characteristics, too. Studies indicate that learning-disabled children have poor social skills and are considered unattractive by their peers. Interestingly, in one study, learning disabled persons overestimated their social acceptance by others probably out of naiveté or as a defence mechanism. When talking to strangers, they appear over aggressive or very diffident. According to Bryan and Pflaum (1986) learning-disabled children fail to read social cues and may misinterpret the reactions of other people. They lack role-taking skills and find it difficult to understand another's point of view. Teachers too tend to rate them negatively even without being told that the child is a learning disabled. Although there needs to be a greater understanding of the social needs of the learning disabled population, not all learning disabled individuals have social difficulties and most grow up to be perfectly well-adapted adults.

References

Blackman, S. & Goldstein, K.M. (1982). Cognitive styles and learning disabilities. *Journal of Learning Disabilities,* 15, 2, 106–115.

Bryan T. & Pflaum, S. (1978). Social interactions of learning disabled children: A linguistic, social and cognitive analysis. *Learning Disability Quarterly,* 1, 3, 70–79.

Kaluger, G. & Kolson, C.J. (1978). *Reading and Learning Disabilities,* Columbus, Ohio: Charles E. Merrill.

Kephart, N.C. (1977). *The slow learner in the classroom* (2nd. ed.). Columbus, Ohio: Charles E. Merrill.

Lerner, J. (1976). *Children and Learning Disabilities* (2nd. ed.). Boston: Houghton Mifflin.

Myklebust, H.R. (1954). *Auditory Disorders in Children: A Manual for Differential Diagnosis,* New York: Grune & Stratton.

Chapter 3

Causes of Learning Disability

Introduction

Research in the area of learning disability has primarily focused on assessment and diagnosis. Research into factors related to etiology, or causes, has been relegated to the background, though there has been a tremendous surge in genetic studies over the past decade. Anxious parents would like to know exactly why their child is not reading or spelling like other children. The general feeling is that if they know what causes a learning disability they may be in a position to prevent it. For the teacher also it is important to be aware of causative factors so that she can choose and implement the appropriate kind of remedial program for that child. Unfortunately, it is not possible to speak of any single factor or group of factors as directly *causing* a learning disability. It is better to speak of *associated* factors rather than seek out *cause and effect* relationships because there are no clearly defined causes. The literature cites many different causes related to a learning disability—organic, biological, genetic, and environmental—but their roles remain ambiguous and tentative. The following section briefly reviews the nervous system and in particular, the structure of the brain as this is helpful in understanding the nature of a learning disability.

The Nervous System

Our nervous system is extremely complex. The most critical period for its development is between the fourth and fourteenth week of gestation during which the foetus is very susceptible to any injury. The nervous system continues to develop after the fourteenth week and into adulthood, increasing in size, maturity and efficiency. The process called *myelination* is important to the development of the nervous system. Myelin is a multilayered fatty tissue that coats the neuron fibres. It helps to protect the neurons and increases the efficiency of neural transmissions. As the brain develops, some biochemical changes are also apparent. The EEG is used to obtain brain wave patterns (measured in cycles per second) which vary from age to age.

Structure of the Nervous System

The nervous system is made up of two regions: (a) the central nervous system (CNS) and (b) the peripheral nervous system (PNS).

Central Nervous System

The central nervous system consists of: (a) the spinal cord, (b) the brain stem, (c) the cerebellum, and (d) the cerebrum (See Figure 3.1).

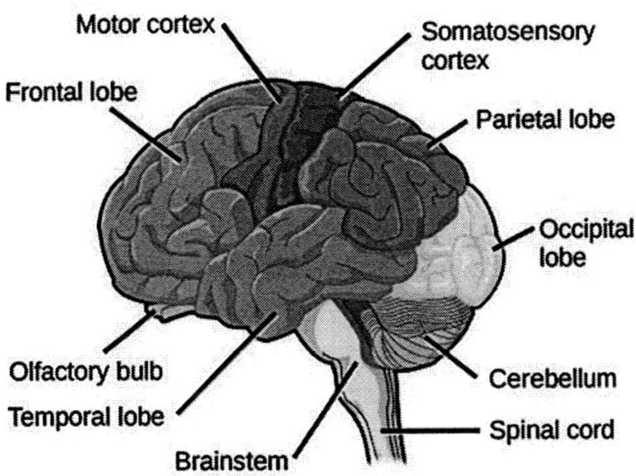

Figure 3.1: Areas of the Brain Associated with Various Functions

(a) The *spinal cord* acts like a relay transmitter carrying information between the brain and the sensory nerves.
(b) The *brain stem* monitors the functioning of respiration, heartbeat and digestion. Together with the upper spinal cord, the brain stem

forms an extremely sensitive network of nerves called the reticular formation (RF). The RF receives and transmits sensory signals to the cortex.

(c) The *cerebellum* regulates voluntary movements, specially fine motor coordination. It is divided into two regions and damage to either side affects the same side (and not the opposite side). Most motor disorders (for example, difficulty in performing a sequence of smooth motor actions, or a poor range of movements) and disorders of speech production are related to damage in the cerebellum.

(d) The *cerebrum* is the largest area of the brain consisting of four regions called frontal, parietal, temporal, and occipital lobes (see Figure 3.1). The outermost layer known as the grey matter (or cerebral cortex) contains neurons, which enable perception, integration of information, thought, and elaboration of motor behaviour.

A great deal of research has dominated the structure and functions of the cerebrum. Of special interest is the work done by Paul Broca (1824–1880) who claimed that speech articulation was governed by the left frontal lobe (this portion of the brain is now commonly referred to as Broca's area). Broca clearly established that the roots of reading—language and reading—originate in the cerebral cortex. Several researchers such as Carl Wernicke (1889) and Alexander Luria (1970) made important contributions that established speech disorders as being linked with damage to the left hemisphere. Carl Wernicke established another area (now called Wernicke's area) that is responsible for understanding language. He discovered that though a patient may speak, it is possible he doesn't understand what is said to him. Receptive language disorders usually have their origin in the Wernicke's region.

These investigations pretty much established that language functions are found in the left hemisphere of right-handed persons and in the right hemisphere of left-handed persons[1]. Whichever hemisphere controls the language functions is called the *dominant* hemisphere. The nondominant hemisphere controls temporal and spatial relationships.

1 *See Chapter 5 for a detailed discussion of brain functions relating to reading.*

Over 90 percent of the population is right dominant. If damage occurs in the developing stages to any hemisphere, the functions of that hemisphere are "relocated." Lenneberg (1967) suggested that before the age of three months both hemispheres have an equal potential for language functions. Cerebral dominance is established between the age of three and five years, but the right hemisphere can adapt to the functions of the left hemisphere up to the age of eleven years. After that there is a loss of plasticity, that is, the ability to accommodate to the functions of the other hemisphere, is reduced.

Peripheral Nervous System

The peripheral nervous system consists of spinal and cranial nerves that are outside the brain and spinal cord and help to connect the Central Nervous System (CNS) with the rest of the body. The peripheral nervous system regulates voluntary, involuntary and automatic body functions.

Normal development can be interrupted in two ways: (1) *by any kind of neurological damage* and, (2) *by maturational delay*. These are discussed below:

1. *Neurological Damage*

Children with learning disability share several characteristics found in persons with brain damage caused by injury or infection. Researchers such as Goldstein, Strauss and Werner studied brain-injured persons (for example, soldiers having head injuries) and found similarities between them and children with learning disabilities. Some of these behaviours were impulsivity, distractibility, figure-ground disturbances, visual-motor disorders, and thinking and conceptual disorders.

Neurological damage can also occur during the prenatal, natal and postnatal periods, resulting in a learning disability. Factors such as *prolonged labour, premature birth, birth complications, maternal age, use of drugs and alcohol, maternal-fetal blood incompatibility, maternal endocrine disorders, Rh-factor, cigarette smoking,* and *low birth weight* are some of the other variables studied. However, it is exceedingly difficult to establish a cause and effect relationship because actual physiological documentation of neurological damage is not easy to obtain. An EEG can be used to establish extent and nature of brain damage. When EEG's were taken from slow readers, some evidence of brain damage was seen such as asymmetry, slow activity, and "sharp waves" in the parietal region. But according to Reitan and Davison (1974, p. 14) brain damage is influenced by (1) laterality of the lesion, (2) site of the lesion within the hemisphere, (3) causal agent (s), (4) individual's age at the time of lesion, and (5) size of the lesion.

2. *Maturational Delay*

Another theory to explain learning disability suggests that it occurs because there is a maturational delay—rather than a permanent dysfunction—within the neurological system. Bender (1973) observed that if differential stages in the development of the brain are delayed, a maturational lag occurs. Some typical symptoms he mentioned (pp.331–333) were:

1. Slow maturation of language skills, specially reading.
2. Delayed development of motor skills.
3. Uneven performance patterns on measures of intellectual development.
4. Visual-motor problems.
5. Incomplete or mixed dominance.
6. Right-left confusion.
7. Immaturity (more often seen in males).
8. Tendency for members within a family to show similar symptoms.

A fair amount of research supports Bender's view that maturational delay is associated with learning disability. De Hirsch (1966) described language deficits of reading, writing and spelling as developmental disturbances, reflecting an immature nervous system. Koppitz (1972–73) in a five-year follow-up study confirmed that learning-disabled children are neurologically immature and suggested that they may need to start school at a later age than other children. Schools must accommodate their programs to meet the child's slower learning rate.

Other Factors

Genetic Factors

The exact nature of the relationship between genetics and learning disability remains obscure but the evidence does suggest that members within a family have a tendency toward learning disability. Hallgren (1950) found that 88 percent of the families of dyslexic children showed similar learning problems. Hermann (1959) examined dyslexia in twins and reported that of the twelve sets of identical (monozygotic) twins, all members were dyslexic. But when the study was conducted with thirty-three pairs of fraternal (dizygotic) twins, only one-third showed both members as being dyslexic and two-thirds had only one dyslexic member.

A lot more recent research is being conducted at centers all over the world. For example, Dr. Lucy Raymond established the Genetics of Learning Disability (GOLD) study in 2001. Her research at the University of Cambridge is focussing primarily on the X chromosome. Dr. Raymond suggests that the most common single gene cause of learning disorder is fragile X, which may account for about 3 per cent of learning disorders in males. She points out that there are many genes involved in learning disability and there is good evidence that as many as 70 genes on the X chromosome may be responsible.

A behavioral-genetic study (called the Colorado Reading Project) of identical and fraternal twins began in 1982 at the University of Colorado by Richard Olson and his colleagues. This expanded in 2001 to include the work being done by Janice Keenan at the University of Denver focusing on deficits in reading and language comprehension. The researchers have initiated a large longitudinal study of identical and fraternal twins beginning at age 4, with follow-up assessments at the end of kindergarten, first grade, and second grade. A major focus of the study is the assessment of preschool twins' learning rate from training for the awareness of abstract phonemes in speech. The study includes international collaborations with parallel studies of identical and fraternal preschool twins directed by Brian Byrne in Australia, and Stefan Samuelsson in Norway.

It should be emphasized that having a genetic risk does not imply that a learning disability is inevitable. The environment mediates all genetic effects. For example, phenylketonuria is a genetic disorder that can lead to severe mental retardation, but restricting the child's diet to reduce the ingestion of an amino acid called phenylalanine can substantially reduce or eliminate the harmful effects of this genetic disorder. Similarly, other forms of environmental intervention can have a significant impact on children with a learning disability.

Biochemical Factors

Chemicals play an important role in brain activity, controlling and releasing electrical nerve impulses between neurons. Absence or excessive amounts of biochemical substances cause a biological imbalance. For example, a delicate balance of acetylcholine and cholinesterase is needed for neural transmission. Metabolic disorders of biogenic amines such as serotonin and dopamine have been of particular interest to researchers. There appears to some relationship between these chemicals and hyperactivity (frequently associated with learning disability).

Nutritional Deficiencies

The developing child requires adequate nutrition, especially so in the first six months. A poor diet and severe malnutrition can reduce a child's ability to learn by damaging intersensory abilities and delaying development. Cott (1972) linked nutritional deprivation to poor biochemical functioning in the brain and suggested a form of treatment called megavitamin or orthomolecular therapy. The treatment which entails daily doses of vitamins and other trace minerals remains controversial but the principle of maintaining a well-balanced diet is sound and pertinent. Though teachers cannot be responsible for their students' diets, they can request parents to improve their child's nutritional needs. Pregnant mothers too must understand the role of nutrition in determining the development of the foetus.

The Role of the Environment

There are several factors in the child's environment which may result in a learning disability. In economically deprived homes, children may not be exposed to adequate sensory, linguistic and cognitive activities. For example, if a child were never given the opportunity to go to school, this would obviously result in the absence of basic academic skills. An emotionally unstable home life may deprive the child of any motivation to learn. Some researchers (Bruner 1971) believe that poor quality teaching in schools can also cause a learning disability. Very often teachers themselves are not equipped to teach a particular subject. A poor teaching style—not giving the learner enough time to acquire basic skills, moving too fast, and failure to understand how best a child learns—can result in learning difficulties of the kind we are describing here.

Fluent Reading is Essential for Enjoyment

References

Bender, L. (1973). Problems of conceptualization and communication in children with developmental alexia. In S. Sapir and A. Nitzburg (eds.) *Children with learning problems: Reading in Developmental Interaction Approach*, pp. 335–349. New York: Brunner Mazel Publishers.

Bruner, E. Teaching disorders (1971). In B. Bateman (ed.), *Learning Disorders* (vol. 4). Seattle: Special Child Publications.

Cott, A. (1972). Megavitamins: The orthomolecular approach to behavioral disorders and learning disabilities. *Academic Therapy*, 7,3, 245–258.

Defries, J.C., Filipek, P.A., Fulker, D.W., Olson, R.K., Pennington, B.F., Smith, S.D. & Wise, B.W. (1997). Colorado Learning Disabilities Research Center. *Learning Disability Quarterly*, 7–8, 19.

de Hirsch, K. & Langford, W. (1966). *Predicting Reading Failure: A Preliminary Study*. New York: Harper & Row.

Hallgren, B. (1950). *Specific dyslexia ("congenital word blindness"): A clinical and genetic study*. Acta Psychiatrica et Neurologica, 65, 1–279.

Hermann, K. (1959). Reading Disability: *A Medical Study of Word Blindness and Related handicaps*. Springfield, Ill.: Charles C. Thomas.

Koppitz, E. (1972–73). Special class pupils with learning disabilities: A five-year follow-up study. *Academic Therapy*, 8, 2.

Lenneberg, V.E. (1967). *Biological Foundations of Language*. New York: John Wiley & Sons, Inc.

Luria, A.R. (1970). The functional organizations of the brain. *Scientific American*, 222, 66–78.

Raymond, L. (2004). Learning disabilities: linking genes to learning disabilities. *ACNR* 4,3,10–20.

Reitan, R. & Davison, L. (1974). *Clinical Neuropsychology: Current Status and Applications*. New York: John Wiley & Sons.

SECTION-II

Kinds of Learning Disability

Chapter 4

Disorders of Language

Mohit's Story

Ten-year-old Mohit was a late talker. At first, his mother thought Mohit's language delay was typical of boys "who talk later than girls," but when he turned four years old, and was still not speaking in complete sentences, she started getting worried. Mohit has now been diagnosed as having receptive and expressive language delays causing "developmental" learning disabilities in the classroom setting. Mohit has difficulty finding words and often uses them in the wrong place. He prefers to use gestures when talking, and tries to avoid verbal communication as far as possible. He is unable to relate events sequentially or describe characters in a story. At best, his responses are limited to three or four words. To the question, "Why was the girl's mother angry?" Mohit would reply, "Door locked." He also has difficulty sequencing the order of words, and letters within a word. For example, he says *nabana* for banana, *tikchen* for kitchen, and "What want you?" for "What do you want?." Mohit reads slowly and is functioning below his grade level.

Mohit has very few friends in school. He tends to get into physical fights and is quick to hit and punch. His classmates tease him on the playground because he is slow to answer back so Mohit uses his fists, which gets him constantly into trouble. He has never been invited for a birthday party. Emotionally, too, he is withdrawn and has lost his bubbly spark. His mother is worried more about his low self-esteem and his difficulties with friends than his academic difficulties.

Language is truly a unique human gift, a complex process that enables communication and social functioning. It remains something of a miracle that by the time a child is four years old, he has mastered the same linguistic system as an adult. Language allows us to express feelings, ideas, and thoughts, to establish relationships with the world in a meaningful way. It is what sets man apart from other species. Through language we can share our experiences with others by describing for them things we have seen, places we have been, or people we have met. Through language we can speak or write about an object without the necessity of having the object present and we can understand an abstract idea with which we have had no personal experience.

Most children acquire speech and language "naturally" in a sequence of listening, speaking, reading and writing. Each skill is built on the preceding one, with "experience" being .the fundamental base or foundation on which the structure of language is erected. However, some children experience serious difficulty acquiring language and are said to have a language delay or a language disorder. In order to fully understand how to help a child with such a disorder, parents and educators must familiarize themselves with some essential components of language. Since language is a complex process, a transdiscplinary approach is necessary. Professionals from different fields—speech and language pathology, special education, sociolinguistics, psycholinguistics and psychology—bring to the study of language a variety of terms, theories, and approaches which can be quite confusing to a parent or teacher. It follows too that often there is no simple explanation for a language disorder nor any one single method that works best.

The Components of Language

Linguists study language as consisting of several interrelated factors: phonology (sound), morphology (word forms), syntax (grammar) and semantics (meaning).

Phonology

Every language is made up of distinct speech sounds or phonemes (in English, there are 43 phonemes). A phoneme is the smallest linguistic unit of speech that signals a difference in meaning. A child learning any language first has to learn the sounds or phonemes of the language. For example, /b/ and /p/ are phonemes that produce two distinct sounds. The phonemic elements in a word are important for a child learning to read. Phonics is the method of teaching reading by attending to sound units of letters. Difficulty in phonological awareness is conclusively related to later difficulties in reading.

Morphology

Morphology is the study of word formation. A morpheme is the smallest linguistic unit with meaning. It may be a prefix, suffix or root word. For example, the word *dogs* is composed of two morphemes—the concept of a dog and the concept of plurality, 's.' Morphemic analysis also looks at grammatical markers such as tenses (ed, ing), and person ('s' is attached at the end of a regular verb, *run*).

Syntax

Syntax is the rule system that governs the structure of a sentence. It specifies word order and sentence structure. The ordering of words within a sentence is critical to meaning. For example, a child must know that "The ball hit the man" is correct, whereas "Ball the man hit" is incorrect. Children who have problems with syntax will face problems in comprehension and usage of language. Syntactic deficits in learning disabled children extend into adulthood. Although research with adult learning-disabled individuals is scanty, a comparative study of the academic performance of learning disabled and non-learning disabled first-year college students, along with a fifteen-year old follow-up study, suggests that differences still remain (King *et al.*, 1982; Wiig and Fleischman, 1980). Wiig and Fleischmann found that the learning disabled students had difficulty in identifying errors and in using third-person plural pronouns, first-person plural reflexive pronouns (ourselves), and relativized sentences. The authors concluded that "...delays in the acquisition of syntax do not recover spontaneously as a function of age-related maturational processes or exposure to more advanced reading materials" (p.50). In telephonic interviews King *et al.* (1982) found that 37 percent of language disordered individuals continued to have chronic language deficits and academic problems in reading English.

Semantics

Semantics is the ability to obtain meaning from words, sentences and other word combinations. A child must know the meaning of words and relationships between words he is using (semantic networks) for him to participate in meaningful conversation.

Pragmatics

Pragmatics is the use of language in social contexts. It also governs the rules of conversation and discourse, for example, greetings, asking questions, answering questions, and requesting clarifications. In order to communicate socially, the speaker must take into account what the listener already knows, and select words and sentences to formulate the appropriate message. For example, it's appropriate to order one's kid brother to fetch a glass, but this would not be suitable if one is talking to a guest. The speaker must know how to use contextual clues, and how to assess a given social situation to make use of language.

It is important to remember that language directly impacts reading comprehension. Reading for meaning and the use of context clues involves the application of higher-level language skills such as knowledge of semantics, syntax and pragmatics. Children who have difficulty in any of these areas will have difficulty with the meaning component of reading comprehension (Nation and Snowling, 1997).

The Development of Language

The development of language has been intensely researched over the past fifty years. It is clearly accepted now that children acquire language in a series of developmental stages. The child's first vocalization is the birth cry, followed by other sounds in the second and third months–gurgling, cooing, and squealing–which resemble consonants and vowels. Typically, when the infant is between 3 and 6 months of age, he begins to babble, that is, to produce sounds such as /ae/, /k/, /m/ and /b/. Babbling has been identified as an important stage in prelingual speech development. Lerner (1976) observed that children with later language disorders often skip this stage altogether.

Around six to eight months of age, the child begins to intentionally repeat his own sounds. This is termed lalling. Some of the common syllables imitated are da-da, ga-ga, and ma-ma. Soon he begins to imitate sounds heard around him (echolalia) but cannot associate these sounds with any meaning.

By the time the child is one year of age, he can utter single words with meaning such as *dada, mama*, and these are quickly followed by two and three-word sentences (*Daddy go, Mummy take* etc.). By age two, most children have a vocabulary of 50 to 100 words or more but what is really distinctive is the ability to combine words into phrases and sentences. By the time the child enters school, he possesses a linguistic system that is essentially the same as adults, except for articulation.

The normal sequence of language acquisition is shown in Table 4.1.

Table 4.1: Stages of Language Acquisition

Period	Receptive Language	Expressive Language
Birth- Six weeks	Involuntary bodily response to sound or crying Listens to sound	Reflexive Cry Differentiated Cry
3 months	Sound Localisation and tracking Smiles when spoken to Differentiated response to individual voices of specific words	Produces sounds for the sake of making and hearing them (coos, gurgles, etc.) Babbles
6–9 months	Responds to his or her name Looks for source of sound	Vocal play with vowel-consonant repetition Use of intonation in language production
10–18 months	Associates words with objects Understands simple commands ("Come here")	Says first recognizable word-usually a noun Can say 8–10 words by 18 months though not distinctly

Period	Receptive Language	Expressive Language
18–36 months	Can understand and respond to two simple requests ("Get the doll and bring it here.") Increases receptive vocabulary from about 100 to 250 words during this period	Practises sound production Rapid expansion of spoken vocabulary Begins to use words to form 2 and 3 word strings during this period Initially uses telegraphic utterances ("Go walk") Ask questions Uses negation ("No bye-bye")
3–5 years	Receptive vocabulary approximately 900 words Associates labels with objects or pictures	Increasing use of speech to express emotions, ideas and needs Begins to classify words into grammatical classes Uses approximately 200 to 300 words by age 4 Mean sentence length is about 4 words
5–6 years	Receptive vocabulary approximately 2,000 words	Begins to use plurals, possessives, and correct verb tense Mean sentence length increases to about 6 words Production of most speech sounds has been mastered
6–8 years	Receptive vocabulary develops from 13,000 to 28,000 words during this period	Mastery of sound production by the end of this period Mean sentence length increases to about 8 words by age 8
8 and beyond	Continued development of receptive vocabulary through direct and indirect experiences	Linguistic performance resembles that of an adult Continued refinement of complex syntactic structures Incorporates newly acquired words into spoken vocabulary according to experiences and situational demands Develops and refines written expression

Source: Learning Disabilities: Understanding Concepts, Characteristics, and Issues. By C. Houck. Prentice-Hall Inc.,1984.

How is Language Acquired?

Theories of Language Acquisition

There are two approaches that explain how language is acquired: the biological or nativist approach, and the behavioural. However, common to both approaches is the basic concept that language is sequential and acquired in stages.

The Behavioural Model

B.F. Skinner (1957) described language as a learned "verbal behaviour" which is acquired by a process of reinforcement and imitation. A baby copies its mother's intonational and speech patterns which in turn get reinforced over continuous interactions. The child continues to repeat the word or phrase when the parent reinforces him. Skinner's behavioural model emphasizes the role of the environment and uses stimulus-response theory to explain how language is used.

The Biological Approach

By contrast, the nativists believe that language is "hard-wired" within the child from the moment of birth. According to Chomsky (1957) language competency is innate. Every child is born with innate linguistic universals that allow him to build a theory of grammar. This in turn helps him to comprehend and produce an infinite number of sentences. Chomsky believes this capacity to generate rules is universally found in every culture.

Lenneberg (1964, 1967) proposed a rather different theory that language has a biological basis. The role of the environment is restricted to providing the child with the raw material to be used for communication. Language is essentially a cognitive process that emerges as the brain matures neurologically and chemically. Since language is based on a unique maturational process, Lenneberg suggested that the optimal period for primary language development is two to twelve years. After the age of 12 (when the brain is fully matured) it is difficult for language acquisition to occur. Lenneberg postulated, "important speech milestones are reached in a fixed sequence and at a relatively constant chronological age" (p. 221).

Other researchers who hold the view that language has a biological basis are Bloom and Lahey (1978); Slobin (1971); and Smith and Miller (1966). Slobin in fact introduced the term "psycholinguistics" and described it as dealing with "the underlying knowledge and abilities which people must have in order to use language...the mental processes that are involved in using language and learning to speak" (p. 2, 1978).

Three major variables emerge as critical to language development. They are: (1) heredity, (2) maturation, and (3) environment. It is not necessary to subscribe to any one particular theory of language acquisition, but it is important to understand how these factors interact when planning a remedial program for students with language disorders (see Table 4.2).

Table 4.2: Significant Variables in Language Acquisition

1.	*Heredity* (a) Anatomical and physiological factors (b) Innate capacity for language learning (assumed) (c) Intelligence
2.	*Maturation* Emergence of "readiness" stages for language acquisition
3.	*Environment* (a) Adult language used with the child (b) Child-rearing practices (c) Peer-group language used with the child

Source: M. Marge. "The General Problem of Language Disabilities in Children," In J.V. Irwin and M. Marge (eds.) *Principles of Childhood Language Disabilities.* Copyright@1972, p. 79. Reprinted by permission of Prentice-Hall, Inc., Englewood Cliffs, N.J.

According to Marge (1972), the acquisition of language is really a synthesis of all the above factors. An individual is born with an innate capacity for learning language, which determines the rate and level of language acquisition. But in addition to this inborn linguistic capacity, maturation of specific brain mechanisms is also essential. The role of the environment, too, cannot be ignored because when a child receives reinforcement for making speech sounds "he may be stimulated to acquire language more rapidly than normally expected" (Marge, 1972, p. 81). As the child progresses into adulthood, all these three factors continue to interact and effect concept formation, problem solving, thinking, academic learning and social interactions.

Understanding the Difference Between Speech and Language

Speech difficulties are usually classified as *articulation* problems. A child may have a disorder such as a cleft lip or palate, which prevents him from pronouncing words or speaking fluently. He may not be able to make the required speech sounds due to motor difficulty. He may have a stammer (also called a stutter), which slows down his rate of speaking. All too often, such children need to have prolonged speech therapy.

Language difficulties usually are indicative of some disorder in the central nervous system that prevents the child from acquiring communication skills. The child may have no difficulty saying the sounds (he can usually repeat words and sentences when prompted), but he may misuse words, or may be unable to recall a word.

Language disorders are usually classified as difficulties in a) receptive language (understanding) and, b) expressive language (speech production).

Receptive language is the ability to understand verbal language. Receptive language disorders have also been termed *word deafness*, *sensory aphasia* and *auditory verbal agnosia* (Orton, 1937; Wepman, 1951; Myklebust, 1954; McGinnis, 1963). Children with deficits in this area will find it difficult to discriminate between speech sounds, and have a poor understanding of word meanings and grammar. They may have difficulty associating names with objects, naming objects, recalling the names of objects, and interpreting environmental language. Some children may repeat words without meaning and this is called echolalia. It is a predominant characteristic of autistic children.

Understanding the meaning of words is another area of difficulty for children with a learning disability. Lerner (1976) observed that children comprehend word meanings in a sequence, moving from concrete to abstract. They acquire the names of objects, actions and qualities before they can understand names of abstract concepts. Words such as *house*, *table*, and *man* are easier to understand than words such as *with*, *the*, and *who*. Comprehension of oral language also requires the use of simple grammar rules and of correctly structured sentences and paragraphs. Many learning disabled children tend to understand words when used in isolation, but get confused when that same word appears in a sentence. Such children also have difficulty understanding idioms, sarcastic comments, long sentences, and ambiguous instructions ("Shouldn't you have closed the door?").

Expressive Language Disorders

Expressive language is the ability to use language to communicate with others. Children with problems of expressive language may comprehend what is said to them but have difficulty expressing their thoughts and ideas. There may be several reasons for this. The child may have motor difficulties (also called aphasia), which inhibit his speech. Spontaneous speech may be limited and the child may use 1–2 word responses. Conversational speech might be marked with gaps and "fillers" ("I mean...uh...you know...that thing to stick paper..."). Or, when a word is retrieved it doesn't express the real meaning, for example, "I like ...uh... pie" (cake). They have a "word finding" problem, and are slow to recall names, labels or events. Grammatical errors may persist.

The two processes of receptive and expressive language are in reality interdependent and cannot be separated. As the child grows older, he needs language to communicate and to understand the world around him.

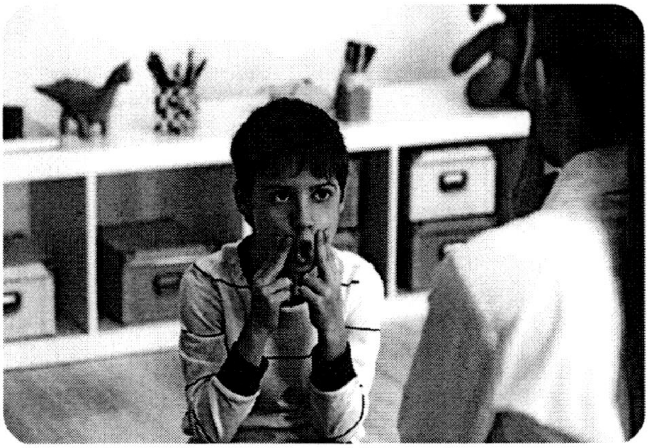

Delay or Disorder?

There is also some confusion between the terms *delay* and *disorder*, which needs to be clarified. A delay is said to occur when the child falls outside the norms of expected development. For example, if a two-year is not speaking 1–2 words, she will be diagnosed as having a speech delay, with the expectation that given appropriate intervention, she is able to close the gaps. However, if the delay continues and impacts the child's understanding and ability to relate to her environment, there is the possibility that the delay is indicative of a more deep-seated, pervasive problem. In such a case, the child is said to have a disorder.

Anything that interferes with a child's ability to communicate with his environment in a normal manner has the potential to cause a speech or language delay. These behaviors include how a child:

- Plays with toys and other children or adults
- Requests or rejects objects or activities
- Greets others
- Imitates sounds and actions
- Understands simple language
- Expresses feelings and emotions

Parents and educators need to be alert to any possible delay so that the child receives appropriate assessments and interventions. Children with speech and language delays are often picked up in the classroom because of their short attention span, difficulty attending in class, and inability to work independently. Failure to accomplish language milestones (see Table 4.1) between 18 and 24 months should be considered a 'red flag.' Many children are late talkers due to a variety of reasons. It could be that there is little or no stimulation at home. However, the delay becomes a disorder when progress slows down to such an extent that the gaps in the child's receptive and expressive language increase. The most common causes of speech/language delay are mental retardation, hearing impairment, autism, cerebral palsy, genetic disorders and brain injury.

The child with both receptive and expressive delays is most likely to have mental retardation or autism. In fact, children with autism are defined as having significant speech and language delays; they have a communication disorder, which affects their social skills. Children with learning disabilities are seldom affected to such an extent. Some of them may show signs of delayed speech and difficulty understanding language but as a group they tend to have milder delays rather than disorders and respond well to early intervention.

Bilingual children or young children who are learning two or more languages simultaneously may show a slight expressive language delay early in their development and will "code switch" (combine both languages), which can also make them appear to be language delayed. However, living in a bilingual/multilingual environment is not a sufficient explanation for expressive language delay.

Dyslexia: A Language Deficit

What exactly is the connection between reading and spoken language? Are late talkers at risk for later reading difficulties? There is a lot of current research to support the view that dyslexia is a manifestation of a deficit in the language system (Simpson, S., 2000).

If one subscribes to the belief that there is a relationship between oral and written language, then any difficulty or delays in phonological skills, word retrieval, speech production, and verbal working memory may affect reading ability. The relationship between reading and phonological processing has been explored in Chapter 5, but it should be mentioned here that any deficits in the phonological processing systems might affect reading fluency.

Paradoxically though it is not true to say that all children with spoken language difficulties will go on to have written language difficulties (reading and writing). Other factors such as the severity and persistence of speech and language difficulties have to be considered, too.

An increasing amount of evidence indicates that a family history of language difficulties (late talking) provides one clear indicator for which children are at-risk for dyslexia (DeFries *et al.*, 1997).

Assessment of Language Disorders

The assessment of language disorders in children is an extremely complex and sensitive task. Parents and teachers should use informal observation techniques and leave the use of formal assessment to speech and language therapists. The fact that language is a complex process makes a transdisciplinary approach very necessary. A child with a language delay may need therapy with a speech therapist (if he is not speaking clearly); a language therapist would help improve his social communication skills and his comprehension; a special educator would assist with academic skills (reading, writing etc.), and so on.

Informal Assessment

Teachers and parents are best advised to use informal procedures because these yield the most helpful information about the child. The first step is to obtain a case history of the child. Questions asked should relate to the child's home background, medical history, social-emotional condition, and any previous remedial programs used. Next, obtain a language sample of the child. This can be a half-an-hour conversation with the child in different settings. The teacher must ensure the child is relaxed and spontaneous in his speech. The language sample can then be analyzed using the Developmental Sentence Analysis (DSA) (Lee, 1974). The DSA is a published procedure to analyze the language sample of children between the ages of 2 years and 6 years 11 months. It evaluates the child's use of grammar and syntax. The scores indicate the child's use of standard English grammatical rules and the scoring procedure is simple. For a more detailed discussion of language samples, the reader is referred to Long and Channell (2001); Hux *et al.* (1993) and Kemp and Klee (1997). Teachers can make their own language scales such as the one in Table 4.3 designed for use with kindergarten and first-grade children. The teacher simply observes the child for a short period of time and notes whether the child has mastered the skill or not. The scale also allows the teacher to plan appropriate intervention, and provides a basis on which to evaluate the child's progress over time. Language scales of the kind illustrated in Table 4.3 can be constructed for every aspect of language ability.

Table 4.3: Language Scale for Assessing Linguistic Abilities

A. Receptive Language 1. When playing a game like "statue," the child is able to stop suddenly when the music stops. 2. When shown pictures, the child can name and produce the beginning sound of 6 out of 10 objects. 3. The child is able to follow verbal directions (use a game like "Simon Says" or simple instructions such as "Touch your nose"; "Close the door"). 4. Given a box of crayons, the child is able to choose the colour named by the teacher. 5. Given a box of ten crayons, the child is able to select the crayons that have the "r" sound in their names (green, purple, orange). *Observations:*
B. Expressive Language 1. Given action pictures, the child is able to make up a story. 2. The child is able to perform simple roles using actions (How does a mother carry a baby? How does the gardener spray the garden?) *Observations:*

C. Memory

1. When shown a picture and told a story, the child can retell the story.
2. The child can follow a series of directions ("close the door, open the cupboard, take out the English reader and open to page 21").
3. The child is able to reproduce a picture drawn (and then erased) by the examiner.
4. When shown a picture, the child is able to recall at least three objects after the picture has been removed.

Observations:

D. Making Associations

1. The child is able to match pictures of objects that go in pairs (bread and butter, horse and carriage, belt and skirt, shoes and socks).
2. The child is able to make simple categories using pictures (things we eat, plants, animals).
3. The child is able to supply answers to three riddles ("He mends our shoes; he is a ________"; "We go to her when we are sick; she is a ________.")

Observations:

Formal Assessment

There are many commercial tests available, some of which come with computer-assisted scoring software that makes scoring accurate and quick. Table 4.4 presents a summary of some of the popular language tests but the issue of reliability and validity, as explained in *Chapter 9*, must be kept in mind when selecting an appropriate test.

Irrespective of which assessment is selected, there are some fundamental issues that must be addressed by any language assessment (Houck, 1984, pp. 270–271). These are:

1. *Test the Hearing:* Very often a general screening procedure fails to detect a mild hearing loss or infections such as chronic otitis media (middle ear inflammation). So it is important that the child visits a qualified audiologist who will test the child's auditory acuity for the entire range of sound frequencies.

Table 4.4: Language Tests

Name (Author of Test)	*Aspect of Language Measured*	*Age*	*Purpose*	*Description*
Peabody Picture Vocabulary Test—Fifth Edition (PPVT-5; Dunn, 2019)	Receptive Vocabulary	4 years-adult	Measures receptive vocabulary, semantics, and word knowledge	Test is untimed and well standardized. Child points to pictures in response to words spoken by examiner. May be administered by teacher. Administration time—10–20 minutes
Test of Language Development (TOLD-5; Newcomer and Hammill, 1977)	Receptive and expressive aspects of vocabulary, syntax, and phonology	4–9 years	Indicates areas of strengths and weaknesses	Short and easy to administer
Test of Early Language Development—Third Edition (TELD-3; Hresko, Reid and Hammill, 2001)	Receptive and expressive language	2–7 years	Identifies language delays; differences between receptive and expressive language scores	Good test to use when planning an early intervention program. Untimed, usually takes 15–45 minutes to administer
Comprehensive Test of Phonological Processing-2nd ed. (CTOPP-2; Wagner, Torgesen, and Rashotte)	Phonological awareness, phonological memory and rapid naming	5–24 years	Identify persons significantly below their peers in phonological abilities.	Helps identify phonological deficits that contribute to difficulty in reading. Administration time—30 minutes
Preschool Language Scale, 2011 (PLS-5; Zimmerman, Steiner and Pond)	Two areas of Auditory Comprehension and Expressive language	Birth-6 years	Assesses deficiencies in receptive and expressive areas	Administration time—less than one hour.
Developmental Sentence Analysis (Lee, 1974)	Expressive syntax in spontaneous speech	2–7 years	To evaluate the grammatical structure of child's spontaneous speech	100 different utterances are taped and analyzed according to length and type

2. *Test for Sound Discrimination*: An important question that assessment must answer is whether the child is generally aware of sounds and able to locate sounds in his environment. Does he get confused when there are too many or distracting sounds around him? Can he identify and discriminate between speech sounds? Does he respond to different levels of pitch, tone, and inflections? Many language-disordered children are unable to attend to auditory stimuli for sustained periods of time and get easily distracted by irrelevant sounds around them, sounds that other children may not notice. For example, the sound of a passing vehicle, the shuffling of papers in a classroom, or the whirring of the fans or air conditioner. A number of standardized tests are available to test auditory discrimination such as the Wepman Auditory Discrimination test (Wepman, 1973), and the Goldman-Fristoe-Woodcock Test of Auditory Discrimination (Goldman *et al.*, 1970).
3. *Test Speech Mechanisms:* It may be necessary in some cases to consult a speech pathologist to check if there is anything interfering with speech production—for example, weak mobility of the tongue, restricted lip or tongue movements, and malocclusions. In some cases loss of teeth could be contributing to poor articulation.
4. *Test for Developmental Language Milestones/General Intellectual ability:* It is important to ascertain if there is any delay or deviated patterns in the child's communication process. Informal observations or formal tests can be used to assess if there are any developmental lags in the areas of both receptive and expressive language. Is there a significant gap between the estimated intellectual ability and actual performance? If no, then the child's language problem is probably the result of reduced general ability. An informal observation of the child's use of communicative behaviour offers a good clue as to whether further testing is needed. Does the child initiate conversation or wait for others? Is the communicative effort spontaneous or laboured? Other characteristics to observe are the use of incomplete sentences, prolonged pauses, rapid speech, mispronunciations, word substitutions, and imprecise vocabulary.

5. *Appropriate Language Models in the Environment:* Dialectal differences could be responsible for a child's poor speech production. This is especially true for children who come from disadvantaged families, have had erratic schooling, or poor exposure to communication skills. If the parents are themselves deaf, it may be possible that the children will have defective articulation due to the absence of a good linguistic model to imitate.

Instructional Remediation

Language is an interactive process and instruction needs to be applied across a variety of settings. Speech and language therapists will have a major role to play in providing intervention to a child diagnosed with a language based learning disability. Activities will focus on oral work, listening skills, auditory discrimination tasks, and training phonological awareness. Teachers will have to work in close partnership with a speech and language therapist and share resources for the benefit of the child.

Three general approaches to language training can be adopted.

1. In the phonetic approach, the child is taught the correct formation of speech sounds, syllables, words and phrases. This is the traditional method used by speech therapists. Behavioural approaches aim to teach language skills directly by using such techniques as imitation, reinforcement, shaping, modelling and prompting. For example, a child would be taught words by looking at pictures or objects and learning to label them.
2. The second approach emphasizes improving the experiential background of the learner so that the relevant concepts and perceptual skills are acquired. Language usage is linked to use of real-life situations. In order to motivate children, and also control linguistic input, work is often centered on an activity or topic, which is of particular interest to the child.
3. The third approach focuses on improving the child's knowledge of grammatical rules. Based on Chomsky's model of language development, children are taught basic sentence patterns and transformations of these patterns.

Teachers may have to use a combination of methods. Often, an eclectic approach is most effective. Here are some good teaching principles, which should be followed when implementing remedial language programs.

1. The child will need a secure environment where skills in listening and oral expression are valued, encouraged and integrated throughout the instructional day—not just during language instruction.
2. Teachers may have to ask the child to repeat instructions to ensure she has understood. Identify sounds, words, or syntactic structures that are confusing and work explicitly on these.
3. Children with language delays may need more physical prompting (rather than verbal prompts) to help them get started.
4. Make certain the instructional activities are relevant and present language as a functional skill instead of a series of fragmented, unrelated subskills.
5. Give the child time to consolidate developing skills, and help her to generalize these skills across different settings—on the playground, in class, and at home.
6. Exemption from a second language may be required. Many schools require their students to choose a second or third language. Children with language delays may get confused with too many different sound structures and should adhere to one language usage.

Instructional Materials

Within a school context, instructional materials for developing language are best purchased commercially. Teachers should select a program that is practical, structured and suited to the child's needs. The benefit of using such ready-made instructional programs is that they are highly structured and targeted for specific deficits. However, since not all parents and professionals may have access to instructional materials, the alternative is to design a simple remedial program. The first step is to teach the child to attend to sounds in the environment. Remember, learning-disabled children have to be taught to listen. Next, teach the child to discriminate between speech sounds. Let him produce words beginning with each consonant and go on to more difficult blends (bl, cl etc.), and digraphs (sh, ch). When teaching word meanings, it is important to provide contextual clues so that the child can learn to "guess" the meaning by looking at words within a sentence. Provide situational experiences so that the child feels encouraged to communicate, using words. Translate the child's gestures into simple, concrete words. Instead of using standard word lists, use toys and manipulative objects or other stimuli natural to that child's environment. Do not be too demanding that the child must use speech: if he is unable to express himself in words, allow him to show you what he means. Above all, the child must always feel that you are really interested in what he is saying. With these guidelines in mind, teachers can design a remedial program and carefully record the child's progress. Remember, ongoing assessment is as much the teacher's responsibility as the professional therapist's.

Instructional Resources

Excellent resources for language materials are available online. Here are some useful websites:

1. www.linguisystems.com. Their most popular and widely used programs are:
   - HELP workbooks for language processing skills.
   - The No-Glamour Language series.
   - SPARC series.
2. American Guidance Services (AGS) www.agsnet.com offers a wide range of speech and language programs such as the Peabody Language Development Kits (Peabody Language Development Kits: Levels P, I, II, and III-Revised (Dunn *et al.*, 1981a, 1981b, 1981c, and 1981d). There are four Peabody language development kits designed for children with ages ranging from 3 to 9½ years. Each kit has 180 daily lessons, which are designed to stimulate receptive, associative, and expressive linguistic and intellectual processes. No reading or writing is involved in the program. The emphasis is on

language experience through activities such as puppets, picture cards, manipulative, and active student participation.

3. www.sraonline.com

   Scientific Research Associates (SRA) publishes the well-known **DISTAR Language I, II, III** (Engelmann & Osborn, 1970, 1973,1975). The DISTAR language series is a highly structured program for developing expressive and receptive language skills extended over 160 lessons per level. Explicit instructions are given for teachers to implement the program. Continual repetition, reinforcement and feedback are attractive features of this program. Level I is designed for preschool students and focuses on "description of objects, instructional words, information and applications." Also taught are concepts such as *before-after*, *some*, and *only*. Level II, which is intended for Class 2, emphasizes opposites, synonyms, analogies, and questioning skills. Level III, for Class 3, focuses on the analysis of written and spoken language.

References

Chomsky (1957). *Syntactic Structures*. The Hague: Mouton.

DeFries, J.C., Alarcon, M. & Olson, R.K. (1997). Genetic aetologies of reading & spelling deficits: Developmental differences. In *Dyslexia: Biology, Cognition and Intervention* (eds C. Hulme and M. Snowling). Whurr Publishers, London.

Dunn (1981). *Peabody Picture Vocabulary Test-Revised.* Circle Pines, Minn.: American Guidance Associates.

Engelmann, S. & Osborn, J. (1970, 1973, 1975). DISTAR. Chicago: Science Research Associates.

Goldman, R., Fristoe, M. & Woodcock, R. (1970). Goldman-Fristoe-Woodcock Test of Auditory Discrimination, Circle Pines, Minn.: American Guidance Associates.

Hammill, D.D., Brown, V., Larsen, S.D. & Wiederholt, J.L. (1980). Test of Adolescent Language (TOAL). Austin, Tex.: Pro-Ed Company.

Hresko, W.P., Reid, D.K. & Hammill, D.D. TELD-3 (Test of Early Language Development—3rd Edition).

Houck, Cherry K. (1984). *Learning Disabilities: Understanding Concepts, Characteristics and Issues.* Prentice-Hall, Inc. Englewood Cliffs, New Jersey.

Hux, K., Morris-Friehe, M. & Sanger, D.D. (1993). Language sampling practices: A survey of nine states. *Language, Speech and Hearing Services in Schools,* 24, 84–91.

Kemp, K. & Klee, T. (1997). Clinical language sampling practices: result of asurvey of speech/language pathologists in the United States. *Child Language Teaching & Therapy,* 13, 61–176.

King, R.R., Jones, C. & Lasky, E. (1982), In retrospect: A fifteen year study of speech-language-disordered children. *Language, Speech and Hearing Services in the Schools,* 13, 24–32.

Lee, L.L. (1975). *Developmental Sentence Analysis: A grammatical Assessment for Speech and Language Clinicians.* Evanston, Ill.: Northwestern University Press.

Lenneberg, E.H. (1967). *Biological Foundations of Language.* New York: John Wiley & Sons, Inc.

Lerner, J.W. (1976). *Children with learning disabilities* (2nd. ed.). Boston: Houghton Mifflin.

Long, S.H. & Channell, R.W. (2001). Accuracy of four language analysis procedures performed automatically. *American Journal of Speech-Language Pathology,* 10, 180–188.

Marge, M. (1972). The general problem of language disabilities in children. In J.V. Irwin and M. Marge (eds.) *Principles of Childhood Language Disabilities,* pp. 75–98. New York: Appleton-Century-Crofts.

McGinnis, A. (1963). *Aphasic Children.* Washington D.C.: Alexander Graham Bell Association for the Deaf, Inc.

Myklebust, H.R. (1954). *Auditory Disorders in children.* New York: Grune & Stratton.

Nation, K. & Snowling, M. (1997). Assessing reading difficulties: the validity and utility of current measures of reading skill. *British Journal of Educational Psychology,* 67, 359–370.

Newcomer, P.L. & Hammill, D.D. (1977). The Test of Language Development (TOLD). Austin, Tex.: Empiric Press.

Orton, S. (1937). *Reading, writing and speech problems in children.* New York: Norton.

Skinner, B.F. (1957). *Verbal Behavior.* New York: Appleton-Century-Crofts.

Simpson, S. (2000). Dyslexia: a developmental language disorder. *Child: Care, Health and Development,* Volume 26, No. 5, 355–380.

Slobin, D.I. (ed.) (1971). *The Ontogenesis of Grammar: A Theoretical Symposium.* New York: Academic Press, Inc..

Smith, F. & Miller, G.A. (eds.) (1966). *The Genesis of Language: A Psycholinguistic Approach.* Cambridge, Mass.: MIT Press.

Wagner, R.K., Torgesen, J.K. & Rashotte, C.A. (1999). Comprehensive test of phonological processing. Austin, TX: PRO-ED.

Wepman, J. (1951). *Recovery from aphasia.* New York: Ronald Press.

Wepman, J.W. (1973). Manual of Administration, Scoring and Interpreting: Auditory Discrimination (rev.ed.). Chicago.

Wiig, E.H. & Fleishmann, N. (1980). Prepositional phrases, pronominalization, reflexivization, and relativization in the language of learning disabled college students. *Journal of Learning Disabilities,* 13, 10, 45–50.

Zimmerman, I.L., Steiner, V.G. & Pond, R.E. (1999). Preschool Language Scale-5, The Psychological Corporation, Harcourt Brace Jovanovich, Inc.

CHAPTER 5

Disorders of Reading: Dyslexia

Amit's Story

When Amit's mother first brought him for an assessment, he was reading at kindergarten level despite being a Grade 3 student. When I asked him to read for me, he picked up a beginning reader and read it through. When I stopped him in the middle of the page, and pointing to a word asked him to read it, he could not do so. I realized he had memorized the whole book! There were other things I noticed about Amit's reading. He read many words backwards such as no as on; and to as ot. He added words and sometimes misread words, which looked quite alike e.g. "look" and "lock," "house" and "horse." He had the most difficulty with two and three letter words such as on, in, at, and saw. He often inserted the 'n' sound when he saw the letter u.

Amit was able to break up the words into sounds but then he could not blend the sounds back into meaningful words. For example, he could say s-e-n-t-e-n-c-e but pronounced this as scientist. When spelling, all the letters were there but out of sequence, for example, house was spelled as hoeus. Even when talking, he would misuse words, for example, say *upside* instead of *outside*. His general knowledge was good, and he could talk for hours about cricket, a sport he clearly loved.

Amit's profile is typical of a child with dyslexia. His mother took a lot of convincing before she started following a systematic reading program at home. She would read out his Science and Social Studies chapters to him, and encourage him to read aloud from a reader that matched his reading age. She used a read, write, and spell program for almost 2 years and now Amit has almost closed the gaps. His school was very supportive, too. His teacher would read out all Math. word problems, and questions on tests and examinations. Amit was exempted from Hindi. He was given extra time on tests but he was too playful to use the extra time. So his teacher decided to accept oral answers on those questions he could not complete during the time limit. She wrote them in for him. Amit no longer needs this amount of support now. He is currently in grade 6 and uses a computer for his tests and examinations. His older brother has recorded his school textbooks so the amount of support he needs is gradually reducing.

Introduction

Reading is an integral part of education and everyday life. It appears to be a skill that given the right opportunities, people acquire almost with effortless ease. However, while oral language is an automatic skill, reading is not. Reading is acquired through a skills based process. Hence, when parents are confronted with a child who has difficulty reading (that is to say, he is *dyslexic*), they react with predictable dismay and bewilderment. Their tendency is to blame the school, the teachers or the curriculum for their child's inability to read. Worse, many parents consider dyslexia to be a kind of mental retardation when in fact just the opposite is true. Individuals with dyslexia are usually of average or above average intelligence. Many famous persons have been dyslexic: Thomas Edison; Harvey Cushing, the noted brain surgeon; Woodrow Wilson; Albert Einstein; George Patton; Rodin, the famous painter; and Nelson Rockefeller, to name just a few. Evidently then dyslexia has been around for a long time and affects individuals from any part of the world, irrespective of their native language.

Dyslexia Defined

Dyslexia, a term coined by Rudolf Berlin of Stuttgart, Germany, in 1887, refers to a specific difficulty in the area of reading. Other terms frequently used are *severe reading disabilities, primary reading disabilities, specific reading disabilities,* and *word blindness.* It has been estimated that of the children who attend school, approximately 10 to 15 percent have some difficulty in reading, and 85 to 90 percent of all learning disabled children have reading problems (Kaluger and Kolson, 1978). Boys with reading problems outnumber girls at the surprising rate of 4 to 1. In fact, dyslexia has become synonymous with learning disability to such an extent that it has been suggested that dyslexia should be used as an umbrella term for all learning disabilities in general.

Several different definitions of dyslexia can be found in the literature. Like other branches of study, definitions of dyslexia have changed and evolved over the years, guided by research and educational practices. Interestingly, the *Diagnostic and Statistical Manual of Mental Disorders (DSM-IV™),* published by the American Psychiatric Association (2006), makes no reference to dyslexia. It does, however, include conditions called "reading disorder," "expressive language disorder," and "disorder of written expression"—all of which might fall under the umbrella of dyslexia.

How does the law define dyslexia? Both the Individuals with Disabilities Education Act (IDEA) and the Code of Federal Regulations for public education name dyslexia as one example of a specific learning disability (see definitions in Chapter 1) but provides no separate clinical definition of dyslexia. For the purposes of this book, the following definition will be used:

> *Dyslexia is a specific learning disability that is neurological in origin. It is characterized by difficulties with accurate and/or fluent word recognition and by poor spelling and decoding abilities. These difficulties typically result from a deficit in the phonological component of language that is often unexpected in relation to other cognitive abilities and the provision of effective classroom instruction. Secondary consequences may include problems in reading comprehension and reduced reading experience that can impede growth of vocabulary and background knowledge.*
>
> Adopted by the IDA Board of Directors,
> Nov. 12, 2002.

Characteristics of the Dyslexic Reader

Over the years, researchers have tried to determine what characteristics the dyslexic readers share as a group. From the large number of studies conducted, the following conclusions can be drawn:

1. The dyslexic reader is more often a boy than a girl. Males outnumber females approximately 4:1.
2. The dyslexic reader has average or above average intelligence.
3. Severely disabled readers often have comprehension difficulties and cannot understand the meaning of a given passage.
4. Members within the family may show similar reading problems.
5. Dyslexic readers tend to be spatially disoriented, with pronounced left-right confusion. This effects the way they perceive words:
   (a) There is frequent kinetic reversals of letters (b-d; flim-film); words (saw-was), and sometimes entire sentences.
   (b) Sounds are confused (empty-entry)
   (c) Concepts are reversed (floor for ceiling; cake for bread; east for west).
   (d) The reader is usually left-handed, and has difficulty telling right from left.
6. There may be poor figure-ground discrimination and motor and visual-motor patterning. Fine motor movements tend to be clumsy. The child may write very untidily with jerky irregular strokes. The letters tend to be poorly formed, irregular and uneven in formation.
7. Speech difficulties are also a typical characteristic of the dyslexic reader. Stuttering, lisping, cluttering is quite common. Delay in learning to talk is often indicative of later problems in reading.
8. There is a tendency to be hyperactive, impulsive and distracted. Most dyslexic readers have a short attention span, and low frustration level. They tend to perseverate (get fixated on words) and lack the ability to scan lines, an ability required for successful reading. They are unable to discriminate between letters and cannot attend to critical features of a word.

9. Dyslexic readers tend to have an inefficient visual memory system, which prevents their reading from becoming *automatic.* They lack reading fluency.
10. Longitudinal studies confirm that severely dyslexic readers continue to manifest severe reading problems as adults, despite intensive remedial intervention (Frauenheim, 1978; Shaywitz, 2004).
11. The dyslexic reader functions 1 grade below expectancy in the primary classes and 2 or more grade levels below in later school years.

Automaticity in Reading Helps a Child with Meaning

What Causes Dyslexia?

The Medical and Scientific Models of Dyslexia

The cause and effect of dyslexia is of increasing interest to doctors and research scientists.

On the research side, many well-known neurologists and scientists have conducted brain research in an attempt to understand how the brain learns to read. Drs. Bennett and Sally Shaywitz, co-directors of the National Institutes of Child Health and Human Development's Yale

Center for the Study of Learning and Attention, are well known for their use of functional magnetic resonance imaging (*f* MRI) to study brain activity during reading tasks. Their work has helped establish the neurological basis for the disorder they call dyslexia. Figure 5.1 illustrates the key brain systems for reading.

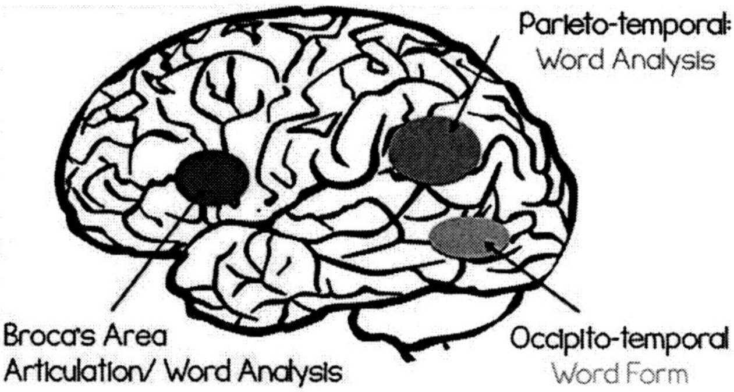

Figure 5.1: Brain Systems for Reading

The Phonologic Model

Researchers such as Sally Shaywitz at the Yale Center describe dyslexia as being a specific weakness in the phonological component of language. Dyslexia reflects a problem within the language system of the brain, which impairs the child's phonemic awareness and doesn't allow him to break the reading code.

Language is processed in the brain by using the phonologic code. The phoneme is the smallest unit of speech that distinguishes one word from the other. There are 44 phonemes that produce thousands of English words. For example, the word cat consists of three phonemes: k, aaa, and t. Before words can be identified, understood or stored in memory they must first be broken down into phonemes by the brain. To read or spell the word *cat*, the reader has to first pull out from his neural machinery the phonemes *k* + *aa* + *t* to say *cat*. Then, he begins to link letters with what he hears in spoken language. He begins to see that the printed word has the same number and the same sequence of phonemes (sounds) as the spoken word. Finally, he comes to understand that the printed word and the spoken word are related. The letters represent sounds. This is called the alphabetical principle and once a child has mastered this principle, he is ready to read.

Shaywitz's (2003, pp. 43–44) research indicates that in children with dyslexia, the phonemes are less well developed. They have difficulty separating words into sound units and fail to appreciate the internal sound structure of words. This explains why they tend to confuse sounds both when speaking and reading. They may retrieve a phoneme which sounds similar to the one asked for, for example, they may say *lotion* instead of *ocean; aminal* instead of *animal.*

Phonemic awareness refers to the ability to notice, identify and manipulate the individual sounds (phonemes) in a word. Once a child grasps the links between phonemes and words, he can decipher the reading code. For most children this process is relatively easy but for others this connection remains a mystery. These children are dyslexic. It is important to remember that phonological weakness interferes with reading but not with comprehension. Phonologic ability is not related to intelligence. This explains why so many bright dyslexic children are difficult to identify. Unfortunately, if a dyslexic reader is unable to read words, his understanding may be affected if he keeps misreading or skipping words.

The relationship between phonemic awareness and reading is now quite well established. Research has clearly established that phonemic awareness is the best predictor of the ability to read words accurately or quickly (Bradley, L. & Bryant, P. 1983). Other experts have found that phonological difficulties are the most consistent and significant markers of dyslexia in childhood.

Some Early Clues of Dyslexia

- A delay in speaking. Generally, children say their first words around the age of one year and start using short phrases by about eighteen months to two years. Children 'at risk' for dyslexia may begin talking much later.
- Difficulty pronouncing words, or persistent baby talk. The child may leave out the beginning sounds (lephant for elephant) or invert sounds (aminal for animal).
- 'At risk' children are less sensitive to rhyme and to the sound structures of words. They have a harder time reciting nursery rhymes and telling if two words sound the same or not.
- Word finding difficulties are an early clue that the child may have later difficulty in reading. The child may use the wrong word (for example, *bun* instead of *biscuit*). He may often struggle to find the precise label, and instead say 'that thing' or 'that stuff' in his daily conversation.
- Difficulty learning the names of letters and their sounds.

Other Approaches to Dyslexia

It is difficult to attribute dyslexia to any one single factor. What was written in Chapter 3 regarding the etiology of learning disabilities in general applies to dyslexia too. It is better to speak of *correlates* rather than causes because there is no distinct cause-and-effect relationship. One of the theories which has received the most attention is Orton's neurological approach that dyslexia reflects a visual-spatial deficit. Research in the area of cerebral (lateral) dominance comprises a very large part of the literature on dyslexia. Orton (1937) observed the tendency in dyslexic children toward reversing letters in reading and writing, and their lack of handedness. He suggested that if cerebral dominance is well developed by the time reading begins, reading proficiency is unaffected. But if there is a lack of dominance (as in the case of dyslexics) reading difficulties occur, showing confused directionality, reversals and mirror images. However, recent research tends to support the phonological model rather than visual-spatial deficit theories.

Research has also examined the relationship between attention and reading disability. Ross (1976) considers learning disability to be the result of "delayed development in the capacity to employ and sustain selective attention" (p.61). Indeed the inability to attend to relevant stimuli is a problem for many dyslexic readers. The efficient reader moves smoothly from perceiving the whole word to individual letters but this is not so easy for the dyslexic reader who shows a tendency to fixate on one aspect of a stimulus just like very young children do. The ability to shift attention and increase the attention span develops with age but this may not always be true for the reading disabled individual.

The inability to read is also associated with inadequate language development. Pearson (1978) observed that when educators forget to look at reading skills in the context of overall language ability and treat dyslexia in isolation, it is a serious error. Reading is directly linked with aspects of language such as vocabulary and word meaning, sentence structure, listening comprehension, and clarity of pronunciation. A failure in any of these areas can lead to a reading disability.

Many educators also consider maturational delay to be associated with a reading disability. "Maturation" refers to the biological, intrinsic unfolding of an individual's potential. Maturation determines the readiness of a child to read. A competent teacher will time her instruction perfectly so that the child is not pushed into reading before he is fully ready. It is also important to select books that match the child's developmental abilities.

How Brain Research Helps Us Understand Dyslexia

Recent brain research has led to startling discoveries that have tremendous implications for understanding learning disabilities. The discovery of CT (Computerized Topography) scans and MRI's (magnetic resonance imaging) in 1973 allowed neuroscientists to look at the structure of the brain for the first time. But it wasn't until the 1980's that scientists could study how the brain actually functions when a person reads, writes, thinks or speaks, due to the use of fMRI (functional magnetic resonance imaging).

Brain imaging studies have also enabled us to better understand the roots of reading and of dyslexia, in particular. Sally Shaywitz and her colleagues conducted studies at the Yale Center for Learning and Attention (USA) asking dyslexic readers to read and took fMRI's as they read. It is exciting to know that we can now record how the brain of a dyslexic reader functions! Figure 5.2 illustrates the difference between a reader with and without dyslexia.

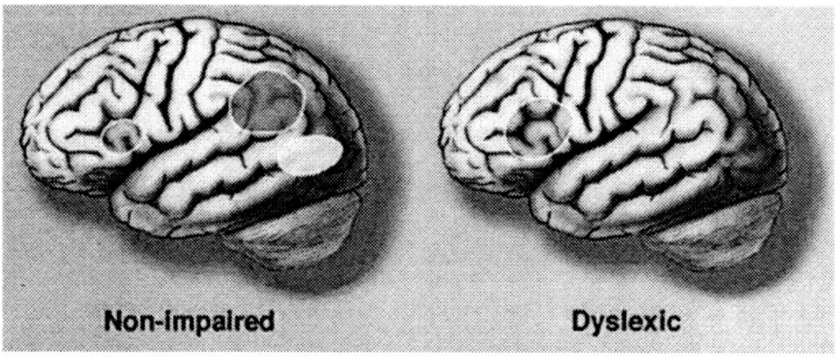

At left, nonimpaired readers activate neural systems that are most likely in the back of the left side of the brain (shaded areas); at right, dyslexic readers underactivate these reading systems in the back of the brain and tend to overactivate frontal areas.

Figure 5.2: A Neural signature for Dyslexia: Underactivation of Neural Systems in the Back of the Brain

Here is a summary of some of their findings, based on imaging studies (Sally Shaywitz, Overcoming Dyslexia, pages 81–89):

1. There are three different neural pathways for reading (Figure 5.1):
   (a) the parieto-temporal and frontal used mainly by beginning readers
   (b) the occipital-temporal, used by skilled readers; and,
   (c) Broca's area in the front of the brain, which helps in slowly analysing a word.
2. Most of the reading part of the brain is in the back. Called the posterior reading system, it is made up of two different pathways for reading. The upper pathway is located mainly in the middle

of the brain (technically, the parieto-temporal region). The lower pathway runs closer to the bottom of the brain (referred to as the occipito-temporal area). This region collects all the information about a word – how it looks, sounds and what it means.

3. Beginning readers use the parieto-temporal region for reading. It allows for a step-by-step approach by the novice reader as he learns to analyse sounds, link sounds with letters, break up words, etc. Skilled readers, by contrast, use the occipito-temporal region at the back of the brain, which responds very quickly to words. This region sees the entire word and automatically recognizes it in less than a heartbeat. This is why the occipito-region is also called the *word form* area. It is not surprising too that the best readers are the ones who rely on the word form area. After a child has read a word many times over and over, he forms a neural model of that word which is permanently stored in the occipito-temporal region. This all happens automatically and spontaneously, with no effort on the reader's part. Practice and experience help to strengthen neural pathways.
4. There is a third reading pathway located in Broca's area in the front of the brain, which helps to analyze words, though very slowly.
5. As they read, good readers activate the back of the brain (with lesser activation in the front) throughout their life. In contrast, dyslexic readers show a fault in the system: underactivation of neural pathways in the back of the brain. Consequently, they have difficulty analysing words and transforming letters into sounds. They remain slow, and not fluent readers, even when they are older.
6. In fact, brain activations in dyslexic children appear to change with age. Imaging studies reveal that older dyslexic readers show increased activation in frontal regions so that by adolescence they are showing an *over-activation* in Broca's area. It is as if they are trying to use the systems in front of the brain to compensate for the disruption at the back of the brain. This helps to explain why many

dyslexic readers subvocalize (say the words under their breath) as they read, a process that means they are using the Broca's area in the front part of the brain. This process of subvocalization allows the older dyslexic student to read although more slowly than if the left posterior systems were working.

7. This pattern of under activation in the back of the brain is universal for dyslexics in all languages and of all ages. Even high-achieving students in University, with childhood histories of dyslexia, continue to show this pattern.

In summary then, brain research has helped us to understand the roots of dyslexia and why reading problems don't go away but persist into adulthood. The key findings are that dyslexic readers use alternative routes to reading. Because they are unable to access the left posterior region, they rely on the right side and frontal systems, which allows them to read accurately but very slowly. They are unable to use an automatic system of decoding because of the disruption in left posterior systems. It also helps to explain why dyslexic readers rely on the use of context (rather than sounds) when reading. They struggle with reading the little words such as *in, on, the, that, an* but can tackle longer words and their performance is better when they have contextual clues. Now that we can see what happens when the brain is activated during the reading process, it would be interesting to see whether we can evaluate the effect of different reading programs on neural pathways.

Assessment of Dyslexia

The purpose of assessment is to provide assistance to the child by fine tuning instruction. Diagnosis must be a carefully planned, systematic, and ongoing process. Standardized tests must be chosen with care and informal procedures devised in a scientific way so as to help in formulating a remedial program. A variety of assessment procedures may be required but the foremost question should be "How can I best help the child?" Teachers may have to collect a wealth of information using direct observations, questionnaires, or interviews, in order to arrive at a sound diagnosis.

When assessing a child for dyslexia, ask:

- Has the child always struggled with reading? The child's family history, developmental factors (such as delayed language) and educational history provide vital clues to later reading difficulties.
- What previous remedial support has been provided? What strategies were most helpful?
- What are the student's current reading habits?
- Does the student demonstrate any peculiar mannerisms when reading (rapid choppy spurts; head movements; loses his place often; uses subvocalizations, etc.)?
- Does the reader use any strategies when reading orally such as breaking up the words, sounding out each letter, and so on?
- Is there any difference in the student's level of comprehension between oral and silent reading?
- Does the child read fluently?
- How strong is the reader's phonological ability?

The diagnosis must establish that the child is not reading at a level commensurate with his age, intelligence, or level of education. Any assessment must also look at both components of reading – decoding (identifying words) and comprehension (understanding the meaning). Younger readers should be able to read *accurately*, and older ones need to be *fluent*. A child who does not read fluently is dyslexic so both fluency and accuracy must be assessed to determine of a child is dyslexic or not. Different tests should used depending on the age of the child, and prior learning experiences.

Some Critical Components for the Assessment of Reading

1. *Test for phonological awareness*[1] *and ability*

With young children, testing must start with an evaluation of phonological skills. Can the child identify if sounds are same or different? Can she produce rhyming sounds? Can the child recognize and manipulate sounds (phonemes)? The ability to decode nonsense words (such as *ip, aff, shep*) is a good indicator of strong phonologic skills in children. Some reading tests refer to this as *word attack.* Research has established that it is very important for children to have mastered their basic phonologic skills by the end of first grade. After that, they continue to build on and refine their knowledge of sounds and apply it to reading.

Most phonological or phonemic awareness tests should include three kinds of measures: sound comparison, segmentation, and blending.

Sound comparison tests require the child to tell which word begins with the same first sound as *rat*: *man, sat,* or *run*. *Segmentation* means asking the child to count or pronounce the individual parts of words. How many sounds can you hear in *man*? (Three). *Blending* is the child's ability to synthesize sounds. You could ask, "What word do the sounds /f/ /aa/ and /t/ make?" (*fat*). In addition, you could ask the child to manipulate sounds. For example, delete part of a word – "Say, *snowman* but drop *man*" (snow). Several tests such as the Phonological Awareness Test and the Test of Word Reading Efficiency (TOWRE) are easy to administer and score. The TOWRE has a subtest of 'nonsense' words, too.

2. *Test for phonologic memory*

It is important to assess the child's ability to store bits of verbal information. Dyslexic children tend to have a poor short-term 'working' memory and take a longer time to remember letter names,

---

[1] Phonologic awareness is a general, all-inclusive term that describes knowledge of sound structures. Phonemic awareness is a more specific term that refers to the ability to notice, identify and manipulate phonemes within a word.

sounds, or number sequences. This type of memory is useful for many academic skills including reading. The child is asked to repeat a series of numbers or words that are presented orally. For example, "Say after me *6–8–9–2.*"

Another type of test called the *rapid automatic naming test* (or RAN) examines *phonologic access,* which is another aspect of phonological processing. The RAN test tries to assess how easily and rapidly a child can retrieve verbal (phonetic) information held in long-term storage. The child is shown a card with several rows of pictures of objects and he is asked to name them one after the other as quickly as he can. Both accuracy and speed are measured. Studies have shown that the faster a child is able to name, the better a reader she is likely to become later on.

3. *Test for knowledge of letter names and letter sounds*

This is a simple test to check if the child knows letters and sounds. Informal or formal tests (that have a section on letter-word identification) can be used.

4. *Test for Reading Comprehension*

Dyslexic readers often do better on tests of reading comprehension than on decoding tests that require them to read a list of single words. This is because when reading a passage, they can use contextual clues, which help with understanding. Carlisle and Rice (2004) point out that no single assessment tool is adequate for testing reading comprehension, because the meaning component of reading is so complex! The assessment must ask a variety of questions such as:

- Does the student understand the text?
- Can he apply ideas?
- Can he retain what he has read?

Poor comprehension in dyslexic children is often the result of decoding problems. If the student cannot read the text accurately and fluently, he will have trouble understanding it. Oral reading tasks (where the passages are read aloud) tend to give more information than those requiring silent reading because the assessor can record errors, note which words are being mispronounced, and so on.

A listening comprehension test is another way of assessing comprehension. The passage is read aloud to a student, and this should result in higher scores than when he is reading silently to himself. Comparing listening and reading comprehension scores is helpful. Teachers can use an Informal Reading Inventory or use standardized reading tests that have both a listening comprehension and a reading comprehension subtest. First graders usually demonstrate better reading comprehension after listening than after reading a text. This is because they are just learning to read words and their limited vocabulary places a limit on the difficulty level they can understand when reading on their own. A very real limitation for older students with reading comprehension problems is that they fall further and further behind their grade level because of their inability to read (decode).

Curriculum-based measures (CBMs) are valid and reliable tools for teachers. Passages are taken from the textbooks so that the teacher can assess performance on what is taught in class (Shin, Deno and Espin, 2000). CBM measures can be administered to individuals or to groups. An oral CBM is typically carried out by asking the student to read aloud a passage from a textbook the child is reading in class. The teacher records errors and marks the passage after one minute, and calculates the number of words read accurately in that time. One problem with this method of oral reading is that it is not an *authentic* reflection of reading comprehension.

Another form of CBM is using the maze task (Shin et al., 2000). A maze task is constructed by deleting every seventh word in a passage and replacing it with three alternatives (one correct and two incorrect alternatives). Students are given 3 minutes to read this passage so speed of decision-making is an important factor. For example:

My mother always likes to go home. She was born on a nice (farm/big/soon) in a valley. Her father started (home/the/sat) farm before she was born. When (red/she/told) was a little girl they lived (to/fun/in) a very old log house on (call/date/the) farm.

(Shin *et al.*, 2000, pg. 166).

Retelling a story is another good way of assessing comprehension. 'Free recall' tasks require students to organize information they have read and this reflects their memory for passage information, expressive language ability, and interpretative skills. Scoring free recall tests can be difficult but the data one obtains is usually very rich and informative.

It's a good idea for schools to have a wide array of tests for assessing reading comprehension as the reading process itself has so many different components. No single test can measure all the different aspects.

5. *Test for reading fluency*

For children in the older grades, and for young adults, a test that looks at reading fluency is important. How does one measure fluency? Shaywitz (2003) provides the following guidelines to help judge a child's oral reading fluency relative to others his age. If the child is reading at a level less than what is given below (the numbers are approximate), he should be considered at risk for reading failure.

Paired Reading Encourages the
Reading Habit and Develops Fluency

Measuring fluency

Grade Level	Correct Words Read per Minute (CWPM)
Grade 1	40 to 60
Grade 2	80 to 100
Grade 3	100 to 120
Grade 4 and above	120 to 180

(Reprinted with permission from Sally Shaywitz, p. 277)

To measure your child's fluency, select a passage from his schoolbooks. It helps to make a copy of that passage so that you can mark his mistakes as he reads. Have him practice reading this till he can read almost every word accurately (19/20 words). Next, time him for one minute as he reads the passage aloud. He should not hesitate over any word for more than three seconds while reading. If he self-corrects within three seconds, mark that word as correct. Add up the number of errors he made while reading. The correct words per minute (CWPM) score is the total number of words read minus the number of errors.

Choosing the Right Kind of Test: Formal or Informal[2]?

Formal Assessment

Standardized reading tests are useful because they indicate how the student is performing compared to students of similar age and ability. Trained psychologists usually administer these tests. As had been discussed earlier in Chapter 1, many countries mandate the use of specific achievement and intelligence tests before the diagnosis of dyslexia can be made. A comparison of ability and achievement scores usually points to a discrepancy, which helps to guide the diagnosis. The child may be under-achieving in specific areas of reading or on a specific ability subtest (Working Memory or Verbal Comprehension, for example), which could indicate reading difficulty.

[2]Standardized tests are often referred to as formal tests. A detailed discussion of the assessment process can be found in Chapter 9.

Table 5.1: Selected Diagnostic Reading Tests

	Name of Test	Age	Components	Estimated Testing Time
1.	Gray Oral Reading Tests-4. PRO-ED, 2001	5 years to adult	Rate, accuracy, fluency, comprehension	20–30 minutes
2.	Woodcock Reading Mastery Tests, AGS, 1987.	4 to17 years	Overall reading ability through reading of a story	20–30 minutes
3.	Woodcock Johnson-IV Tests of Achievement (WJ-IV)	4 years to adult	Letter-Word Identification Reading Fluency Oral Comprehension Passage Comprehension	25 minutes
4.	Wide Range Achievement Test-3, PRO-ED, 1994.	5 years to adult	Single Word reading	10 minutes
5.	Comprehensive Test of Phonological Processing in Reading (CTOPP). PRO-ED, Inc.	5 years to adult	Phonemic awareness Phonemic memory Rapid Naming	30 minutes
6.	Test of Phonological Awareness (TOPA). PRO-ED, Inc.	5 to 9 years	Letter-sound correspondence Phonological processing	10 minutes
7.	The Phonological Awareness Test (PAT) Linguisystems)	5 to 7 years		
8.	Test of Word Reading Efficiency (TOWRE). PRO-ED,1999.	6 to 25 years	Sight words Nonsense words	5–10 minutes
9.	Wechsler Individual Achievement Test-II (WIAT-II). Psychological Corporation, 2001	4 years to adult	Reading, writing and math.	90 minutes

Informal Assessment

Most schools and parents may not have the resources to purchase formal tests as they can be quite expensive. Informal testing is an equally (if not more) reliable method of identifying the child's strengths and weaknesses. For this teachers need to be familiar with the reading process described earlier so that they know what areas of reading skills to assess. Checklists and record forms can be used during classroom observation. Table 5.2. describes a typical observation form for recording reading skills. Using this form, a teacher can test both oral and silent reading. The child's progress can be monitored at regular intervals.

An Informal Reading Inventory (IRI) is another instrument, which helps to estimate the child's general reading level. The IRI is a series of sequentially graded reading paragraphs taken from one book. Unlike a standardized test, where the child is tested with reference to other children, the IRI provides an overview of the general level of reading competence. A good informal reading inventory has been published by Ekwall, E. and Shanker, J. (2000).

Most IRI's use three reading levels:

1. Independent Level – the child reads with hardly any difficulty. Materials are read with 99% accuracy in word recognition. Reading comprehension is usually no less than 90%.
2. Instructional level – the child reads with some difficulty, usually recognizing words with 95% accuracy, and comprehending at least 75% of the given passage.
3. Frustration level – reading occurs with considerable difficulty (usually the child recognizes 90% of the words) and loss of meaning (he comprehends less than 50% of what is read).

Some IRI's have a fourth level to measure listening comprehension.

The IRI is an easy-to-construct assessment tool that also helps in planning the remedial program. However some experts feel that the criteria for determining IRI reading levels are arbitrary, and may be too high.

Teachers can also make their own materials based on published instruments. The "test" should ideally consist of a number of graded

Table 5.2: Reading Assessment Checklist

NAME ____________ GRADE ____________

TEACHER ____________ SCHOOL ____________

No.	1st check	2nd check	3rd check	Item	Area
1				Word by word reading	ORAL READING
2				Incorrect phrasing	
3				Poor pronunciation	
4				Omissions	
5				Repetitions	
6				Inversion of reversals	
7				Insertions	ORAL SILENT DIFFICULTIES
8				Substitutions	
9				Basic sight word not known	
10				Sight vocabulary not up to grade level	
11				Guesses at word	
12				Consonant sounds not known	
13				Vowel sounds not known	
14				Blends, diagraphs or diphthongs not known	
15				Lacks desirable structure analysis	SILENT READING
16				Unable to use context clues	
17				Contractions not known	
18				Fails to comprehend	
19				Unaided recall scanty	
20				Response poorly organized	
21				Low rate of speed	
22				High rate at expense of accuracy	OTHER RELATED ABILITIES
23				Voicing-lip movement	
24				Inability to skim	
25				Inability to adjust reading rate to difficulty of material	
26				Written recall limited by spelling ability	
27				Undeveloped dictionary skill	
28				Inability to locate information	

1st check / 2nd check / 3rd check /

The items listed above represent the most common difficulties encountered by pupils in the reading programme. Following each numbered item are space for notation of that specific difficulty. This may be done at intervals of several months. One might use a check to indicate difficulty recognized or the following letters to represent an even more accurate appraisal.

D – Difficulty recognized

P – Pupil progressing

N – No longer has difficulty

passages (which are unfamiliar to the reader) along with four or five comprehension questions. These questions should have items that measure recall of specific details in a given passage, vocabulary, and inference. The length of the passage and the level of difficulty should be chosen keeping in mind the child's age and achievement levels. Passages of 100 words are used for the beginning reading level and up to 300 to 350 words for the more advanced readers. Teachers should begin testing at a level that is at or slightly below the child's level of current independent performance. If the teacher cannot decide where to start testing, she can use a graded word list. When the child's reading falls below the frustration level, she should stop presenting the graded passages. The next passage should be presented to check listening comprehension. This stops when the comprehension capacity falls below 75 percent. While the student is reading, the teacher should note the errors made as this will help in planning a remedial program. Table 5.3 presents a recording system for oral reading errors.

Table 5.3: Recording System of Oral Reading Errors

Miscue	Marking	Comment
Mis-pronunciation	went (*want*)	The student attempts to pronounce the word but produces a nonsense word, rather than a real word.
Substitution	want (*went*)	The student substitutes a real word that is incorrect.
Refusal to pronounce	TP (*went*)	The student neither pronounces the word nor attempts to do so. The teacher supplies the word so that the testing can continue.
Insertion	sent (*on*) to	The student inserts a word that does not appear in the text.
Omission	to (*the*) school	The student omits a word but continues to read.
Repetition	In the *the* little house	The student repeats one or more words that have been read.
Reversal	No on saw was	The student reverses the order of words or letters.

Source: Paul C. Burns and Betty D. Rose, Informal Reading Assessment. Copyright @1980 by Houghton Mifflin Company. Used with permission.

Another informal assessment instrument is the Reading Miscue Inventory (RMI, Goodman and Burke, 1970). The RMI offers a qualitative analysis of the reader's miscues or errors made during oral reading. Goodman believes that errors are an indication of the child's underlying language structures and need to be analyzed carefully according to graphic, syntactic, or semantic characteristics. The reader is asked to read a complete selection or story followed by a retelling of the story in his own words (this takes about fifteen to twenty minutes). The passage should be selected in such a way that a *minimum* of twenty-five miscues is made – this will allow the teacher to identify the kind of reading strategies used. The reading is recorded so that the miscues can be later analyzed. This in fact is the most time-consuming part.

Here are some useful questions to ask when doing a miscue analysis:

- *Dialect.* Is a dialect involved in the miscue?
- *Intonation.* Is a shift in intonation involved in the miscue?
- *Graphic similarity.* How much does the miscue look like what was expected?
- *Sound similarity.* How much does the miscue sound like what was expected?
- *Grammatical function.* Is the grammatical function of the miscue the same as that of the word in the text?
- *Correction.* Is the miscue corrected?
- *Grammatical acceptability.* Does the miscue occur in a structure that is grammatically acceptable?
- *Semantic acceptability.* Does the miscue occur in a structure that is semantically acceptable?
- *Meaning change.* Does the miscue result in a change of meaning?

The Cloze Technique

The Cloze procedure (Bormuth, 1968) is very popular because of the simplicity of its design and because teachers appear to use it in the normal process of teaching to evaluate comprehension skills (also called a *fill in the blanks* activity). The reader is given an unfamiliar passage in which every fifth word is omitted and replaced by a blank (starting from the second line). The reader has to supply the missing word. If the reader fails to supply 40 percent of the responses, the passage is too difficult. Figure 5.3 describes the cloze procedure.

Robinson Crusoe looked out to sea. Yes, there was a ____ (ship) coming. Robinson Crusoe ran ____ (down) to the beach, calling ____ (and) waving as he went. ____ (He) lit his fire to ____ (signal) the ship. The Captain ____ (saw) the signal and stopped ____ (the) ship.

Figure 5.3: The Cloze Procedure

Some advantages of the cloze procedure are:

- it is easier and quicker to construct, administer, score and interpret than the IRI
- it's use requires less expertise
- it can be group administered
- it provides a good measurement of the ability to use semantic and syntactic cues.

However, one must remember that the cloze procedure provides diagnostic information limited to word recognition, decoding skills and comprehension.

Teaching Reading to the Dyslexic Reader

The reading journey can be a painful and laborious one for dyslexic readers. Most schools in India focus largely on content and teachers know *what* to teach. But it is equally important to know *how* to teach, and the right teaching methods can make all the difference to a child's success or failure. Teaching a dyslexic child is hard work and teachers need to be constantly learning, reading up new research and experimenting with different programs. Instruction has to suit each child's individual needs. By the time a child is firmly diagnosed as dyslexic, he is usually in grade 6 or 7 and is expected to deal with vast quantities of information. Lack of motivation is yet another hurdle because most students have a history of prior failure and hate to read. The teacher must be sensitive to the student's learning style, age, and interests, and choose materials that are suitable to the particular child. There is no fixed formula that works best or any magic ingredient that will instantly help the student to read! But with drill, practice, and appropriate materials a great amount can be achieved.

There are many different approaches to teaching reading, each defined by its own theory and conceptualization of the reading process.

Essentials of a Successful Reading Program

In order to remediate reading difficulties, the quality of instruction must be of the best quality. It is sometimes better to use a ready-made reading program such as Reading Mastery or Open Court Reading than try to prepare a potpourri of skills. Research has established that the following factors effectively contribute to a child's success in reading.

Start Early

If your child has begun to struggle with reading, don't wait to get help. Even though you may not be fully convinced that your child is dyslexic, it is important not to waste time. A dyslexic child who gets no help till he has entered grades two or three is going to have to work very hard to close the gaps. Why wait till he falls further and further behind and loses self-esteem?

Instruction Must Be Intense

Brain research has clearly established that poor readers need frequent and intense exposure to the written word. Ideally, instruction should occur in small groups of three or four, at least four or five times a week. The remedial program must be tailored to the child's specific needs and instruction must be explicit.

Instruction Must Be of High Quality

Teaching reading is a science and teaching dyslexics to read is even more of a perfect science. The responsibility of delivering a high quality program falls squarely on the teacher. She needs to be experienced in reading methods and know how best to motivate her students. Teaching needs to be explicit and systematic. Shaywitz (2003, page 262) points out that the essentials of an effective early intervention program are:[3]

- *Systematic and direct instruction in:*
    - (a) phonemic awareness – noticing, identifying and manipulating the sounds of spoken language
    - (b) phonics – how letters and letter groups represent the sounds of spoken language
    - (c) sounding out words (decoding)
    - (d) spelling
    - (e) reading sight words
    - (f) vocabulary and concepts
    - (g) reading comprehension strategies
- *Practice* in applying these skills in reading and writing
- *Fluency training*
- *Enriched language experiences*: listening to, talking about, and telling stories.

The Program Should Be of Sufficient Duration

Dyslexic readers need at least ninety minutes of reading instruction every day over a period of one to three years. It is interesting to note that a child's reading growth is greatest in the early school years and decreases with each following grade. A child also progresses more rapidly at the beginning of each school year and then tapers off towards the end of the school year.

---

[3] Each of these areas is discussed in detail later in this chapter.

The Reading Journey

Reading is a two-way process involving both recognition of a word (decoding) and understanding (comprehension). Dyslexic readers may have deficits in one area or both. A full understanding of the reading process will enable teachers to plan an appropriate reading program for the dyslexic child.

Teach Phonemic Awareness

Phonemic awareness is the fundamental building block for reading. Recent research has confirmed that phonemic awareness – the ability to identify and manipulate the sounds of language – is a key element in learning to read (Adams, 1990; Smith, Simmons, & Kameenui, 1995). A phoneme is the smallest functional unit of sound. There are 44 phonemes in the English language, including letter combinations such as /th/. For example, the word *cat* contains three distinctly different sounds. The ability to identify the different sounds that make words and to associate these sounds with written words is critical for dyslexic readers.

Children must learn to attend to the sounds of the language in order to read and spell. Word play involving segmenting words into their constituent sounds, rhyming words, and blending sounds to make words is also essential to the reading process. Many children with learning disabilities have deficiencies in their ability to process phonological information. Thus, they do not readily learn how to relate letters of the alphabet to the sounds of language (Lyon, 1995). Children from a non-English speaking background may have particular difficulties with phonological awareness. Exposure to language at home, exposure to reading at an early age, and dialect, all affect the ability of children to understand the phonological distinctions on which the English language is built. Teachers must be sensitive to their needs and use a variety of techniques to help children learn these skills when Standard English is not spoken at home.

Teaching phonemic awareness requires only about 15–20 minutes daily. Activities such as rhyming words, breaking sounds, combining sounds etc. help children understand how words can be pulled apart or brought together by sounds. Practice also helps to build the neural circuitry that links the sounds of letters to the printed letter. Most good quality kindergarten reading programs develop this skill by using rhyming songs, action songs, etc. Direct the child's attention to whether sounds are similar or different? How many parts does a word have? Dyslexic readers may not be able to distinguish between sounds and tend to confuse words which sound alike such as *bag/beg*; *pit/pet*; *pin/pen*.

Examples of phonological awareness tasks (Stanovich, 1994) include:

- ***Phoneme deletion*** – "What word would be left if the /k/ sound were taken away from *cat*?"
- ***Word to word matching*** – "Do *pen* and *pipe* begin with the same sound?"
- ***Blending*** – "What word would we have if we blended these sounds together: /m/ /o/ /p/?" (*mop*)
- ***Phoneme segmentation*** – "What sounds do you hear in the word *hot*?"
- ***Phoneme counting*** – "How many sounds do you hear in the word *cake*?"
- ***Rhyming*** – "Tell me all of the words that you know that rhyme with the word *cat*?"

Work on Words (Decoding)

After a child has developed phonemic awareness, he is ready for the next step in the reading process – taking words apart and putting them together. Pulling apart a word into its sounds is called segmenting. Pushing sounds back together is called blending. These are the two main skills required for both reading and spelling.

Most reading programs for kindergarten students begin by teaching children how to break up words into big chunks of sounds, syllables, and then introduce the smaller pieces, phonemes. Syllables are the largest unit of sounds that make up a word and are easy for children to identify and play around with. A good dictionary generally gives the number of syllables in a word. A simple activity that encourages 'syllabification' is asking children to count (or clap) the number of syllables in their name. For example, the name *October* has three syllables: Oc... to... ber and would need three claps.

The next step, separating syllables into phonemes, is much harder, especially for those children who are dyslexic. Sound matching games are a fun way to start. Ask the child to identify the beginning sound in a word, and later the ending sound. Show a picture of a cap, say clearly "This is a *kkkap*." Ask him to name the picture. Next say, "The first sound in cap is *kkk*. Can you say the first sound?" Then lay out four or five picture cards, some beginning with the *k* sound. Ask him to say the names of each of these pictures and then to group all the objects beginning with the *k* sound. You can add other sound matching games to this activity. For example, ask the child "Is there anything in the room that begins with a kkk sound?"

Once a child is good at matching sounds, teach him *segmenting* or how to pull sounds apart. Ask him to add a sound and see what word it makes. For example, "What would *cap* become if you add sss to it?" Or, take away a sound from the beginning, ending or middle positions. "Can you say *post* without saying ttt?"

The next step, *blending* sounds, is perhaps the hardest for young readers. You can ask the child, "What word makes the sounds you hear: 'zz' 'ooo' (zoo)?" Use concrete objects such as blocks or coins to help him see that the word *zoo* is made up of two sounds.

Resources for Teachers to Stimulate Phonological Awareness:

- Phonemic Awareness in Young Children: A Classroom Curriculum (Paul Brookes). Suitable for kindergarten, first grade and special needs children.
- Phonological Awareness Training for Reading (PRO-ED), kindergarten through grade two.
- Road to the Code (Paul Brookes), kindergarten and first grade.
- The Lindamood and Lindamood Reading program
- Jolly Phonics – www.jollylearning.co.uk

- DaisyQuest and Daisy Castle (kindergarten and first grade)
- Earobics (preschool through elementary). Published by Cognitive Concepts.

From Phonemic Awareness to Phonics

Phonics is an organized method of teaching children all about the relationship of letters to sounds. How do different sounds combine? What rules apply? Are there any exceptions to the rules? To be most effective, phonics instruction should start as early as kindergarten and continue into first grade. Phonics help to improve a child's spelling and comprehension. It gives the child a powerful tool that he can apply to any new words. The traditional phonics approach has often been criticized as being boring and repetitive. Teachers often wonder whether it is necessary to teach phonics. There has never been any doubt about the effectiveness of phonics, but it should be taught properly. Many good phonics programs are available in the market and teachers should select a program that is both systematic and explicit.

Here is the sequence in which phonics should be taught:

1. Single consonant sounds – m, t, s, f, d, r, g, l, h, c, b, n, k, v, w, j, p, y.
2. Vowel sounds – first short vowels, then long vowels.
3. Complex letter-sound patterns: once a child has mastered some consonant-vowel combinations, introduce digraphs that is, when two letters represent one speech sound. For example, sh-as in shop, ch – as in chip, – ng as in thing; and wh – as in what.
4. Rules – Starting first grade, children are taught that the sound of a letter may depend on what letter comes after it. For example, a vowel followed by a consonant and then an e is pronounced as a long vowel. For example, take, cake, fine etc. This is also called the 'silent e' (or magic e) rule. Rules encourage children to examine a word closely and are a good way of explaining non-phonetic English words.

Expanding Reading

After first and second grade, children learn to read longer and more complicated words. They continue to build upon their early knowledge of phonics and need access to a different set of strategies to pull apart complex words. For example, the fourth or fifth grader can break up a multi-syllabic word into smaller chunks, using natural breaks that occur in the word. Or, he can be taught to recognize the root of the word. How are words built? Does a word have a pre-fix or a suffix? For example, the prefix *un* means *not*, so *unprepared* means *not prepared*; *unlikely* means *not likely* and so on. Knowing the roots of a word helps the child to pronounce it, spell it, and recognize it's meaning. For example, – *ology* means *'the study of'* and knowing this allows the student to decipher difficult words such as biology; zoology, etc.

Teaching Sight Words

Sight words (sometimes called irregular words) are words that don't seem to have any specific rules to guide the reader how they should be said. They are words that don't have a specific pattern. For example, *said, been, could, are, the, is* etc.

The only way to teach sight words is to memorize them. Introduce the word, use it in a sentence, write it out, and ask the child to say it. Then ask her to write it out again. Printing each word on a card helps the child commit it faster to memory (which is why they are called *flash cards*). It is important to choose:

- words with high utility,
- words which occur most often in the language,
- words needed often in writing, and
- words the child almost knows and that a little more practice will bring to overlearning.

Appendix 1 lists the 220 Dolch Basic Sight Words that are words most frequently encountered in a text. They make up twenty five percent of all words appearing in print. Review a few words every day. Remember, practice is the key to becoming a skilled reader. The Dolch list can also be downloaded from www.theschoolbell.com

Words in Context

Older dyslexic readers encounter complex reading materials and tend to rely more on *contextual clues* when reading. Contextual clues are 'words in context,' and include syntactic and semantic cues. Syntax is the arrangement of words in sentences and a syntactic cue allows the reader to examine word order and guess what the word says. If the reader has information about how a word should be used in a sentence, it increases his ability to derive meaning from the sentence and read correctly. For example:

The man is wounded
The man wound the clock

Let's assume *wound* is the unfamiliar word. In the first sentence, the position of wound in relation to the other words indicates it has to be an adjective. In the second sentence, it is a verb. Some prior knowledge of grammar and rules is of course essential for the reader to use syntactic cues.

A semantic cue is the ability to derive meaning from the words in the text and they work in much the same way. For example:

Every w________ it snows in the mountains.

Clearly the missing word is *winter* because in the context of the total sentence, it is the only word that makes sense.

Some general points about using words in context should be noted. The reader must have some knowledge of the meaning of the words in his oral vocabulary. Contextual cues function best when the reader has extensive background knowledge to draw upon so that the process of "filling in the blanks," as it were, is efficient and quick.

Another kind of word clue is called *structural analysis*. The reader is able to break up an unfamiliar word by analyzing its structural features. He examines the meaningful elements in a word by looking at the root word, prefix, suffix, word-endings (ing, ed), contractions and so on.

The overall context of a sentence often helps a reader to guess at the correct word. Dyslexic readers have special difficulty with word meanings and will probably take longer to recognize semantic clues. Steiner, Wiener, and Cromer (1971) observed that poor readers "seem to be identifying words as if the words were unrelated items unaffected by syntactical or contextual relationships." Specific training in the use of contextual clues will be very useful for such readers. Context clues help students to (1) identify words they previously identified but forgot, (2) check the accuracy of words tentatively identified by the use of other clues, (3) rapidly recognize a word because they can anticipate what the word might be, and (4) identify words that are not identifiable in any other way.

Teaching Fluency

Fluency acts as a bridge between decoding and comprehension. First, a child learns to read a word accurately, and then with repeated practice, he is able to read those words fluently with good pronunciation and understanding. The child merely has to glance at the word to fire the neural circuitry in the brain and instantly know what the word is. At least four correct readings are required for a dyslexic reader to *automatically* recognize a word. Accuracy does not evolve naturally into fluency. This is especially true for the dyslexic reader who may read accurately but may never learn to read fluently.

The National Reading Panel analyzed a hundred research articles on fluency and concluded that there are three key approaches that yield the maximum gains. These are (a) the child must read loudly, (b) he must be given opportunities for practice, and (c) ongoing feedback must be provided as the child reads. The most important advantage of loud reading is that it allows the child to correct his pronunciation of words and helps him to store the correct neural model of that word in his brain. Silent reading does not do this. When a child reads aloud, it allows the adult to give him immediate feedback. Experts refer to this approach by different names such as guided repeated oral reading, repeated reading, paired reading, shared reading, and echo reading. It takes about 15 minutes per lesson, and can be used by a teacher, parent or tutor. The teacher first models by reading a paragraph aloud and then the student reads the same paragraph aloud. The child reads that passage again at home with parents gently correcting his mistakes. The next day, students pair up with each other and take turns reading to each other.

The material selected for guided oral reading must be comfortable (not too hard, not too easy), since fluency builds on accuracy. Books must be at the child's independent reading level, that is, the child should be able to read 19 out of 20 words correctly.

The best way a parent can help their child develop fluency is to set aside twenty minutes every evening and ask the child to read out loudly. Try to get a duplicate copy of the book so you can take turns reading. Unfortunately, the child who is a poor reader is also the one who hates reading so it's important that you help your child break this cycle. The dyslexic reader reads too little and needs to "overlearn" words. Overlearning is the result of repetition, drill, and practice. Practice means rereading the paragraph at least four times (this need not be all in one session). Since practice may stretch over months, parents need to build in some incentives to encourage the child. Graphing the child's progress enables him to see concrete evidence of his improvement.

Parents and teachers can order programs specifically designed to improve fluency. Read Naturally (www.readnaturally.com) has a set of twenty-four non-fiction stories on CD-ROM, for students reading at grade one through grade seven. *The Open Court and Language!* Reading programs also have units that teach fluency training (see Appendix 1). In the Reading Recovery program, there is a strong emphasis on teaching for fluency and phrasing in oral reading. In the 30-minute Reading Recovery lesson, the majority of time is devoted to students' reading of continuous text.

Fluency training can also be used to teach a list of single words. This is called speeded word training. The child should be able to name words at the speed of less than one second per word or at least sixty words per minute. The word can be written on a flash card; or, five to six words can be written on a larger card. Word lists for speed drills can be obtained from Oxton House Publishers at www.OxtonHouse.com. Many of these lists are suitable for older children, too.

Poems are another excellent way to increase fluency because they are short, have rhyme, and can be read quickly. Students can sit in a circle and read selections from a play. Lyrics from a song are particularly good when the teacher wants the whole class to read together (choral reading). For students in the higher grades, extract key words across subjects such as science and social studies and use these as a word list.

Parents often wonder how they can help their child become a better reader. There is probably no better way than using this method of guided repeated oral reading to develop fluency training. It is simple, requires little or no expertise, and takes up just about twenty minutes every day. Yet its effects are powerful because it allows the child to build up the correct word models in his brain. Once a child can decode quickly, he can do a better job of concentrating on the meanings and spellings of words.

Reading for Understanding

Books are meant for enjoyment and knowledge. As a child moves into the higher grades, the material increases both in quality and quantity. The extent to which a child can understand what he reads depends not just on his ability to pronounce the words but also on his knowledge of word meanings or vocabulary. By the beginning of third grade, a child will start encountering new unfamiliar words in his books, words he may not use when speaking. How does one build up vocabulary? Simply learning the meanings of words does not help. Words stand for ideas and students have to be taught different words to express ideas. The new word has to become a part of the child's daily experience. For example, if the new word is 'culture,' ask him to generate some ideas about what the word culture suggests to him. Encourage him to use that word in sentences and then to go beyond to incorporate it in his daily life.

A child's vocabulary grows by about three thousand new words a year. Children hear new words all around them, when they visit the shopping malls, watch a television show, and so on. Only a small proportion of a child's vocabulary comes from direct instruction. What implication does this have for teaching?

1. Teachers need to carefully select the vocabulary words they want the child to learn. They should choose words the child is not likely to get on his own. If the student is reading a story, select words relevant to his understanding of that story.
2. Select words that relate to a common theme. Words can be integrated into categories such as 'words that arouse fear'; 'words that describe a fight' and so on. Forming of categories helps children incorporate these words into their own thinking when reading and writing.
3. Encourage children to bring new words into the classroom and award a prize to the child who comes up with the most new words. Remember, children need the new words to be repeated over and over again for them to remember what it means.

Learning-disabled children have difficulty with both *literal* and *interpretive* comprehension skills. *Literal comprehension* is the recall of directly stated facts. It involves skills such as noting details and facts, understanding words and paragraphs, recalling a sequence of events, identifying the main idea and skimming a passage to locate a specific detail. Difficulties with literal comprehension arise from the inability to understand the meaning of words – most learning-disabled children spend so much time trying to decode a word that it affects their ability to derive meaning. Many children also find it difficult to select the meaning of homonyms (like waist/waste). Children with limited experiential backgrounds are particularly weak in this area. Grasping the main idea is also difficult for them because they are unable to find the central theme in the mass of details. The length of a passage may also affect their understanding of the main idea.

Interpretive comprehension is the ability to make analytical judgments, state a point of view, make inferences and evaluate what is read. These "higher thinking skills" are often lacking in children with a learning disability. The mechanical aspect of reading (decoding) places a heavy demand on the memory and slows down their ability to use inferential skills. Sometimes if a passage is read out to the student, there will be a dramatic improvement in his ability to answer interpretive questions about what he has read. In order to be able to draw conclusions, make comparisons between ideas, and integrate new ideas with old ones some explicit training in thinking skills may be required.

One excellent strategy is to preview the chapter or book with the student before he even opens the book. Discuss the title and ask the student to predict what he thinks the theme will be. The teacher should identify any key ideas and difficult words the student may encounter. After the book is open, establish the structural outline right from the start. Ensure that the student has grasped the who, *what, where, when* and *why* of the narrative. As the student reads, ask him to identify the main idea of a paragraph or chapter; summarize the key issues; ask him to retell in his own words the sequence of events. After the book is complete, ask him to reflect on the characters and express his opinions about the book.

> *Resources for Reading Comprehension*
>
> Assessing and Teaching Reading Comprehension: Practical Strategies That Work, By Miriam Trehearne. She has also published The Comprehensive Literacy Resource for preschool Teachers (2004) and a sequel for grades 3–6 in 2005 (ETA/Cuisenaire).

Some Specific Reading Problems and How to Remedy Them

When teachers refer a child who has been having difficulty reading, they simply say, "Anjana cannot read." However, it is important to specify the exact nature of the reading errors so that the remedial program can focus on the particular deficit. Dyslexic children demonstrate some very specific error patterns that may continue into adulthood.

Errors in Reading

1. *Omissions*: The reader omits letters (for example *belt/bet*) or whole words when reading. Generally, it is the middle and ending part of a word that is omitted, so the child's attention must be directed

to special features of the word. Teaching him to scan the complete word is a useful strategy.

2. *Additions* and *insertions*: the reader inserts a letter where not required (*play/played*) or a syllable (*care/careful*). This happens because he fails to follow the context, is unable to identify the words quickly, or fails to comprehend the meaning of what he is reading. Choral reading and having the child read along with a recording can help.
3. *Substitutions*: the reader substitutes words, which look the same (*house* for *home*; *guess* for *guest*). There is a great deal of wild, meaningless guessing (*bus/ biscuit*). The child focuses only on the initial part of the word and ignores the rest. It may be that the child is over-relying on configuration cues and ignoring the context. He probably has a poor sight vocabulary and inadequate word-recognition and decoding skills. Mispronunciation, which is also a form of substitution, could be the result of poor auditory discrimination, undetected hearing or vision defects, poor syllabification and phonics skills.
   The use of flash cards is a good method to remedy substitutions because it directs the student's attention to the sounds and syllables of individual words. Teach the child how to tackle new words when he comes across them in a passage. Some children feel they have to read very fast without interruptions and so they substitute any word that they can think of, rather than trying to analyze the word and the context. To remedy mispronunciations, use diacritical markings with the child. Teach the child to listen for sound differences. Practice with choral reading and rhyming also helps.
4. *Repetitions or regressions*: A child frequently repeats words because he cannot make sense of the meaning or is embarrassed and nervous when reading. The end result is a very slow, erratic rate of reading. Regressions occur generally because the child feels a need to verify what was read, he missed the meaning in the sentence, or there is lack of confidence.

One way to correct regressions and repetitions is to ask the child to first read silently before reading aloud. Use phrase cards instead of a passage which may appear overwhelming to the child; develop a stock of sight words which he can read fluently; have the child listen to himself read so that he realizes he is repeating words.

5. *Reversals:* Orton first introduced the term "reversal" to explain how learning-disabled persons twist symbols when reading and writing. Letters, parts of words, or whole words may be reversed, for example, *p* and *q*, *b* and *d*; *was* for *saw*; *aminal* for *animal.* Sometimes an entire part of the sentence is reversed: "*The boy went into the garden*" becomes "*garden into the went the boy.*" Or, part of a compound word gets transposed: *postman* becomes *manpost.* Letters within a word may also get inverted when reading: *me* becomes *we*; *bad* becomes *bag*; *bun* is confused with *bus*.

   Orton suggested that reversals indicate inadequate cerebral dominance and some kind of defective neurological organization. More specifically, there is a perceptual disorder that reflects a developmental delay or deficit. Another group of researchers attribute reversals to a lack of figure-ground discrimination, that is, the child is unable to perceive spatial relationships. However, perceptual errors of reversals are very common among kindergarten children (as high as 90%) and children grow out of this usually by the age of seven. If the tendency for reversals persists into Grade two and three, both in terms of duration and intensity, it indicates a more serious problem. Moyer and Newcomer (1977) suggested that reversals occur because the child is unfamiliar with the concept of directionality and the problem is one of letter sequencing. Table 5.4 lists some words most commonly reversed. Most young children reverse letters and words when introduced to reading and writing in the Nursery and Primary classes. The difference is that a dyslexic child continues to do so well into the higher classes and the frequency of the occurrence is also much greater. With repeated instruction, normal children outgrow the orientation confusion held responsible for such reversals, but a learning disabled child takes much longer to overcome the problem.

Table 5.4: Commonly Reversed Words

was	pin	no	pal	rats
step	tubs	pot	on	nip
saw	trap	net	tip	lap
tap	rat	part	pot	star
pan	ten	top	snap	pit
cop	but	pat	tar	pets

The elimination of reversals is a challenging task because they are very resistant. The first step is to establish the concepts of right and left by using motor movements. Teachers can use a simple game like "Simon says raise your right hand up." Next, teach them to distinguish between letters that circle to the right (B, P,p,b,h,m,n,r) and circle to the left (c,a,d,q,e,f). Use colours if needed. Direct their attention to the fact that reading involves sweeping from left to right. Other methods (see the use of The Magic Ruler) are described in Appendix 1.

6. *Word-by-word reading*: The dyslexic reader frequently loses his place when reading, using no intonation, expression or punctuation, and pausing so long that he loses sight of the meaning. Poor word-identification skills, lack of a sight vocabulary and inability to use context are some common causes to explain word-by-word reading. Some remedial tips are: increase the pace of the reading by moving a piece of paper along the page; read along with the child at a faster pace; use flash cards with phrases; give the student practice in choral reading.
7. *Sound Blending.* Dyslexic readers may continue to isolate the sounds while reading even in much older grades, producing what teachers will recognize as a very slow, laborious rate of reading. Some children may know the individual sounds but yet find it

difficult to combine those sounds into words. Problems with visual and auditory discrimination often lead to difficulty in blending sounds. Bannatyne (1973) observes that sound blending must become automatic so that the child does not focus entirely on "coding" the word and can attend to comprehension as well. It is important to remedy this problem by teaching meaningful word patterns (rather than emphasizing isolated word sounds) and using words in context.

8. *Memory Skills.* Children with reading disorders often have a poor memory and are unable to: a) retain impressions or traces of visual and auditory stimuli; b) make comparisons with past auditory and visual experiences; and c) store and retrieve grapheme-phoneme correspondences (Chalfant and Scheffelin, 1969). Children with auditory memory disturbances may not remember words, or letter sounds. On the other hand, a child with poor visual memory may not recognize specific letters and words. Since memory is dependent upon storage and retrieval of information, the problem could lie in either of these two areas. Children with reading disability may also be suffering from an attention deficit disorder (ADD) or hyperactivity (ADHD). Poor memory effects their ability to recall the order of letters in a word and the sequence of words in a sentence. The result is scrambled words for example, *chrai* for *chair*, *mlik* for *milk*, *jetkac* for *jacket*. Visual sequencing problems are common among learning disabled children and often persist longer than other deficits.

Auditory sequential memory disturbances may give rise to omission of initial consonants (the child reads *member* for *remember* or *uitcase* for *suitcase*) or distortion of the sequence of sounds (the child reads *lowbe* for *below*). Teachers must note the frequency of errors and the kind of omissions or distortions the child makes as this will form the basis for appropriate remediation.

Other General Approaches

Fernald Method Grace Fernald (1943) popularized the multisensory approach, often referred to as the V-A-K-T because it uses Visual-

Auditory-Kinesthetic-Tactile strategies. The V-A-K-T method is briefly described below:

1. A word is selected from a word list.
2. The teacher writes the word (using either manuscript or cursive writing) on paper or the board.
3. The teacher reads out the word, the student repeats it.
4. The student traces each letter with the finger or a pencil until he can write it from memory.
5. The student writes the word without looking at the model.
6. The new word is typed out and included in the student's wordlist.

With practice, Step 3 is eliminated and the student merely looks at the word, repeats it and writes it down. At a more advanced stage, the student may not need to have each word

The Orton-Gillingham Method

This method uses a phonics method for teaching reading (Gillingham and Stillman, 1973). The system involves auditory, visual, kinesthetic and tactile stimulation. The student looks at a letter, hears the teacher say it, and then repeats it. This three-step procedure is also called the *language triangle.* The later stages closely resemble the Fernald method with the student tracing a letter formation and then writing it from memory. The Orton-Gillingham method lays down strict conditions about the sequence of activities presented in their manual. Special training is necessary for use of the program.

The Davis Method

It was in 1980 that Ron Davis described his program for correcting dyslexia in adults and children in his book entitled The Gift of Dyslexia. The Davis Dyslexia Correction program is suitable for children age 8 and over, and adults of any age. The program has two main approaches. First, it teaches dyslexic students how to recognize and control the mental state that leads to distorted and confused perceptions of letters, words and numerals. Second, it gives dyslexic students the ability to think with symbols and words, so they can learn to read easily and with full comprehension. Using clay, students first work with the alphabet, numerals, and punctuation marks, to make sure that they have an accurate perception and understanding of these symbols. Students then use clay to model the *trigger words*—the short abstract words, frequently encountered in reading, such as *and, the, to,* or *it.* These words cause problems when dyslexic students cannot form a mental picture to go along with them. Through **Symbol Mastery**, the student makes a three-dimensional clay model of the meaning of each word, together with a model of the letters of the words. With this approach, learning is considered to be permanent.

References

Adams, M.J. (1990). *Beginning to read: Thinking and learning about print.* Cambridge, MA: MIT Press.

Bannatyne, A. (1973). *Reading.* San Rafael, Calif.: Academic Therapy Publications.

Bormuth, J. (1968). *The cloze readability procedure.* Elementary English, 43, 1968, 429–436.

Carlisle, J.F. & Rice, M.S. (2004). Assessment of Reading Comprehension, pp. 521–540. In *Handbook of Language and Literacy: Development and Disorders.* Ed. By C. Addison Stone, E.R. Silliman, B.J. Ehren, K. Appel. The Guilford Press.

Chalfant, J.C. and Scheffelin, M.A. (1969). Central processing dysfunctions in children: A review of research (NINDS Monograph No. 9). Bethseda, Md.: U.S. Department of Health, Education, and Welfare.

Ekwall, E. & Shanker, J. (2000). Reading Inventory, 4th Edition (ESRI-4).

Fletcher, J.M. (1994). Cognitive profiles of reading disability: Comparisons of discrepancy and low achievement definitions. *Journal of Educational Psychology,* 86: 6–23.

Goodman, Y.M. and Burke, C.I. (1970). *Reading miscue inventory: Manual procedure for diagnosis and remediation.* New York: Macmillan.

Heilman, A.W. (1977). *Principles and practices of teaching reading (4th.ed.).* Columbus, Ohio: Charles E. Merrill.

Johnson, M.S. & Kress, R.A. (1965). *Informal reading inventories.* Newark, Del.: International Reading Association.

Johnson, D.J. & Myklebust, H.R. (1967). *Learning disabilities: Educational principles and practices.* New York: Grune & Stratton.

Kaluger, G. & Kolson, C.J. (1978). *Reading and learning disabilities* (2nd. ed.). Columbus, Ohio: Charles E. Merrill.

LaBerge, D. & Samuels, J. (1976). Towards a theory of automatic information processing in reading. In H. Singer and R. Ruddell (eds.). *Theoretical Models and Processes of Reading* (2nd.). Newark, Del.: International Reading Association.

Moyer, S.B. & Newcomer, P.L. (April, 1977). Reversals in reading: Diagnosis and remediation. *Exceptional Children.*

Pearson, David P. (1978). Some practical applications of a psycholinguistic model of reading. In *What Research has to say about Reading Instruction.* ed. S. Jay Samuels. Newark, Del.: International Reading association.

Ross, R. (February, 1966). Teaching the listener: Old mistakes and a fresh beginning. *The Elementary School Journal,* Vol. 66, 239–44.

Shin, J., Deno, S.L. & Espin, C. (2000). Technical adequacy of the maze task for curriculum-based measurement of reading growth. *Journal of Special Education,* 34, 164–172.

Slosson, R.L. (1963). Slosson Oral Reading Test. East Aurora, N.Y.: Slosson Educational Publications, Inc.

Steiner, R., Wiener, M. & Cromer, W. (Dec. 1971). Comprehension training and identification for poor and good readers. *Journal of Educational psychology,* Vol. 62, 506–13.

Woodcock, R.W. (1973). Woodcock Reading Mastery Tests. Circle Pines, Minn: American Guidance Service.

Kameenui, E.J. (Winter, 1996). Shakespeare and beginning reading: The readiness is all. *Teaching Exceptional Children,* 27(2).

LaBerge, D. & Samuels, J. (1976). Towards a theory of automatic information processing in reading. In H. Singer and R. Ruddell (eds.). *Theoretical Models and Processes of Reading* (2nd.). Newark, Del.: International Reading Association.

Moyer, S.B. & Newcomer, P.L. (April, 1977). Reversals in reading: Diagnosis and remediation. *Exceptional Children.*

Pearson, David P. (1978). Some practical applications of a psycholinguistic model of reading. In *What Research has to say about Reading Instruction.* ed. S. Jay Samuels. Newark, Del.: International Reading association.

Ross, R. (February, 1966). Teaching the listener: Old mistakes and a fresh beginning. *The Elementary School Journal,* Vol. 66, 239–44.

Shaywitz, Sally (2003). *Overcoming dyslexia.* Albert A. Knopf.

Smith, S.B., Simmons, D.C. & Kameenui, E.J. (February, 1995). Synthesis of research on phonological awareness: Principles and implications for reading acquisition. (Technical Report no. 21, National Center to Improve the Tools of Education). Eugene: University of Oregon.

Stanovich, K.E. (1994). Romance and reality. *The Reading Teacher,* 47, 280–291.

Steiner, R., Wiener, M. & Cromer, W. (Dec. 1971). Comprehension training and identification for poor and good readers. *Journal of Educational psychology,* Vol. 62, 506–13.

Williams, J. (1971). Learning to read: A review of theories and models. In F. Davis. *The Literature of Research in Reading,* Vol. 4, pp. 429–453. New Brunswick, N.J.: Rutgers University.

Woodcock, R.W. (1973). Woodcock Reading Mastery Tests. Circle Pines, Minn: American Guidance Service.

Associations

Division for Learning Disabilities (DLD) The Council for Exceptional Children 1920 Association Drive Reston, VA 22091 703/620–3660.

Learning Disabilities Association (LDA) 4156 Library Road Pittsburgh, PA 15234 412/341–1515.

National Adult Literacy & Learning Disabilities (ALLD) Center Academy for Educational Development 1875 Connecticut Avenue, NW Washington, DC 20009 202/884–8185.

National Center for Learning Disabilities (NCLD) 381 Park Avenue South, Suite 1420 New York, NY 10016 212/545–7510.

Orton Dyslexia Society 724 York Road Baltimore, MD 21204 800/222–3123.

The following Internet sites provide additional information on students with disabilities: www.ldonline.org

Chapter 6

Disorders of Written Language (Dysgraphia)

Anjali's Story

Ten-year-old Anjali has never enjoyed writing. When she was in kindergarten, her teachers noticed that she had difficulty remembering the shape of the alphabets, and would often say, "My hand hurts." Her spellings have always been poor and the overall quality of her handwriting is almost illegible. When asked to copy short sentences from the blackboard, she writes very slowly and seldom completes her work in class. Her oral responses are clever and sharp but she is unable to put her thoughts down on paper. She makes grammatical errors, uses few or none punctuation marks, and drops out words in sentences. Anjali indicates all signs of having a writing disorder or dysgraphia. Here is Anjali's writing sample:

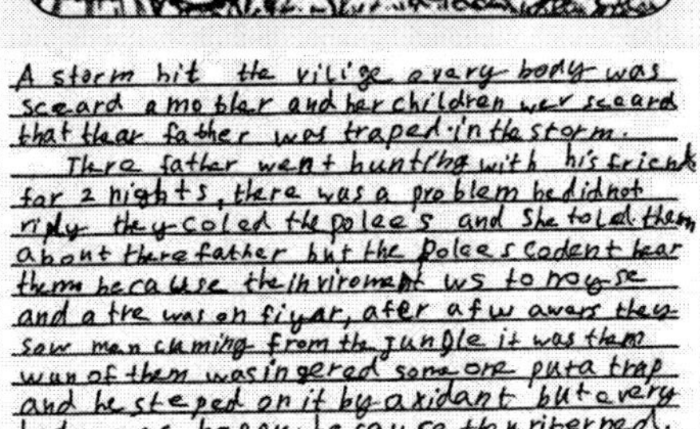

A storm hit the vilige every body was sceard a mother and her children wer sceard that thear father was traped in the storm.

Thre father went hunting with his friend for 2 nights, there was a problem he didnot riply they coled the polee's and She told them about there father but the polees codent hear them because the invironment ws to noyse and a tre was on fiyar, after a fw awars they saw men cuming from the jungle it was them wun of them was ingered some one puta trap and he steped on it by axidant but every body was happy because they riterned.

Raja's Story

Seven-year-old Raja began walking "much later than his brothers and sisters" and his mother, Mrs. Kapur, described him as being "a clumsy child." "He was always bumping into tables or chairs, dropping stuff, and hurting himself" she said. Till now, Raja is afraid of coming down the stairs and needs help to button his shirt. Raja hates drawing and writing. His paper usually has holes in it from constant erasing. He writes many letters backwards and sometimes entire words. Raja finds it very hard to copy from the blackboard. He said that he looks at a word on the board and then looks down to write it. When he looks up again to write the next word, he can't find where he was in the note and spends time searching the whole board for it. A chalky, dusty board makes it hard to read because, "My eyes go different and I have to focus again."

Usually, the teacher makes him stay in at recess until it's done. If it's still not finished, he has to finish it at home.

Mrs. Kapur was relieved when Raja was finally diagnosed as having dysgraphia. The teacher started doing things differently in class. She would make Raja copy from a sheet of paper instead of from the blackboard. His parents ordered an Alpha Smart (a writing device that is similar to the keyboard of a computer) and Raja are thrilled to use it in class. "It gives me choices when I am spelling words" said Raja excitedly and added, "My paper looks very neat and clean. I can even read back what I write."

Introduction

Writing is the most important form of communication and in the hierarchy of language abilities; it is usually the last to be learned. Written language allows us to communicate with each other, to express ideas and feelings, and share knowledge. In school, the quality of written expression demonstrates that the student has mastered concepts, and measures academic learning in tests. Unfortunately, what is often overlooked is the fact that writing is a complex skill that requires coordination of several abilities. A piece of writing reflects how ideas move from the writer's mind and are shaped into a carefully laid-out design where each word has to be selected and sequenced accurately, otherwise it would make no sense to the reader. It is hardly surprising that writing is not the favourite pursuit of many students. Youngsters who are already struggling with the content matter of their textbooks may not be able to master the intricacies of the writing process. For learning disabled students, writing is a skill they may never master and often, they get labeled as being 'lazy'; 'not interested'; and 'slow.'

Disorders of written language are referred to as *dysgraphia* and this include difficulties in three areas: (1) handwriting (2) spelling and, (3) content. An important challenge is how to determine the severity of the problem. When is the problem severe enough to be called dysgraphia? After all, poor handwriting, inconsistent spellings and irregular letter formation are complaints that teachers make about almost every school-going child. When should a parent take these complaints seriously enough to call the child *learning disabled?* What if the problem is not intrinsic to the child but due to poor teaching, or to English being the child's second language? A good starting point is to understand all the elements that enter into writing; and, the appropriate developmental stages. This can help us determine whether or not there is cause for serious concern.

Ideally, a good school curriculum should go hand in hand with the developmental stages for writing. Unfortunately, this is seldom the case as most schools expect children to write even before they have the necessary muscle control!

Table 6.1 outlines the sequence in which writing skills develop.

Table 6.1: Developmental Hierarchy of Writing Tasks

I. Scribbling
II. Tracing: a. Connected letters of figures b. Disconnected letters or figures
III. Copying: a. From a model b. From memory c. Symbolic and nonsymbolic
IV. Completion tasks: a. Figure b. Word completion-supply missing letters: 1. Multiple-choice 2. Recall c. Sentence completion – supply missing word
V. Writing from dictation: a. Writing from letters as they are spoken b. Writing words and sentences c. Supply missing word d. Supply missing sentence
VI. Propositional Writing.

Source: Central Processing Dysfunction in Children: A Review of Research by J.C. Chalfant and M.A.Schefflin, NINDS Monograph No. 9. Bethseda, MD.: US Department of Health, Education and Welfare, 1969, p. 112.

Jordan (1977) identified six key characteristics associated with dysgraphia and these are listed in Table 6.2. The checklist is helpful as it covers the three main areas of written language – handwriting, spellings, and the content. Usually these are interlinked problems and it is expected that a child having difficulties in any one of these areas may experience a spillover in the others, too.

Table 6.2: Checklist of Dysgraphia Characteristics

Difficulty with Alphabet Symbols

- Does not remember how to write certain letters or numerals
- Distorts shapes of certain letters or numerals
- Overall writing effort is awkward, uneven
- Has difficulty transferring from manuscript to cursive style
- Continues to print manuscript style long after introduction to cursive style
- Fragments certain letter or numeral forms
- Writing resembles 'bird scratching,' is virtually illegible
- Has difficulty distinguishing between capital and lowercase letter forms
- Mixes capital and lowercase forms

Confusion with Directionality

- Writes certain letters, numerals, or words in mirror image
- Tends to write on mirror side (left side) of vertical midline when moving to next column
- Marks from bottom to top when forming certain letters or numerals
- Uses backward (clockwise) motions when forming loops in certain letters or numerals
- Erases or overprints habitually to change directions of certain letters or numerals
- Writing tends to slant up, down, or to wobble up and down

Sentence Structure

- Composes meaningful content in spite of poor handwriting
- Transposes grammatical elements within sentences, but produces good overall meaning
- Tends to use complete sentence forms instead of fragments

Difficulty Copying Simple Shapes

- Distorts simple shapes
- Fails to close corners
- Tends to draw "ears" where lines meet or change direction
- Has difficulty reproducing simple designs from memory
- Work deteriorates towards end of writing exercise
- Has difficulty staying on lines when tracing.

Tendency to Telescope
- Omits letters when writing words
- Omits syllables or sound units when writing words
- Runs letters together
- Runs words together (usually when copying).

Tendency to Perseverate
- Adds unnecessary letters or sound units to written words
- Repeats the same letters or syllables in written words
- Adds unnecessary sound units to spoken words
- Repeats syllables or sound units in spoken words
- Falls into parrotlike repetition of naming word units during games or conversation

Source: D R Jordan, Dyslexia in the Classroom (2nd ed.). Columbus. Ohio: Charles E. Merrill Publishing Co. 1977, pp 6667. Reprinted by permission of the publisher.

Pushing Children to Write Early May Increase their Frustration

Disorders of Handwriting

Most learning-disabled children hate to write and avoid it wherever possible. Lack of motivation becomes a real obstacle, and a teacher needs to be at her creative best when encouraging a learning disabled child to write. No formal criteria are available to clearly define what 'technically' constitutes a handwriting disorder, and this can be confusing. Some common types of handwriting errors (listed in Table 6.3) act as a useful guideline for parents and teachers.

Table 6.3: Common Handwriting Errors

Defect	Causes
1. Too much slant	a. Writing arm too near body b. Thumb too stiff c. Point of nib too far from fingers d. Paper in wrong direction e. Stroke in wrong direction.
2. Writing too straight	a. Arm too far from body b. Fingers too near nib c. Index finger along guiding pen d. Incorrect position of paper.
3. Writing too heavy	a. Pressing index finger too heavily b. Using wrong type of pen c. Penholder too small in diameter
4. Writing too light	a. Pen hold too obliquely or too straight b. Eyelet of pen turned to side c. Penholder too large in diameter.
5. Writing too angular	a. Thumb stiff b. Penholder too lightly held c. Movement too slow.
6. Writing too irregular	a. Movement lacks freedom b. Movement of hand too slow c. Pen gripping d. Incorrect or uncomfortable position.
7. Spacing too wide	a. Pen progresses too fast to right b. Excessive, sweeping lateral movement.

Source: Educational Assessment of Learning Problems: Testing for Teaching. By G. Wallace and S.C. Larson Boston: Allyn & Bacon, 1978. Copyright 1978 by Allyn & Bacon, Reprinted by permission.

Causes for Handwriting Errors

There are many reasons why a child could have problems in handwriting. Usually, there are a combination of factors such as lack of developmental readiness, visual-perceptual weakness, and confusion with directionality.

Poor Readiness Skills

The absence of prewriting skills is one major reason why some children fail to write correctly. In the normal course of development, a child develops sufficient muscle control before the second year to grasp crayons or other writing tools and to produce random scribbles. With time, the child is able to hold a pencil with three fingers and by age five he has the fine motor control necessary for prewriting activities. He is also able to attend to visual stimuli and discriminate between features like size, shape, and spatial orientation. Early problems with writing, for example, reversing letters (d is written as b), letter size, problems with spelling, and incorrect movements are gradually self-corrected, as the child grows older.

However, for some children this normal course of development is delayed. Motor development and coordination may be slow. Children who have not had the experience of squeezing, twisting, and manipulating objects may find it difficult to control a crayon or pencil. Fine motor coordination is a very essential prerequisite for writing. Children lacking fine motor control tend to hold the writing tool very tightly or too loosely. Unless corrected quickly, this may develop into a writing disability when the child enters school.

Children in kindergarten and grade 1 should typically be able to perform the following 10 tasks:

1. Print in a left-to-right sequence.
2. Easily use three fingers to grasp the pencil tip.
3. Write the first name (manuscript or cursive).
4. Maintain proper position and posture.
5. Draw (copy) a triangle, which has three distinct angles.
6. Copy a common word from a near-point model.
7. Draw a human figure with recognizable head, body, arms, and legs.
8. Copy a word from a far-point model.
9. Stay on the lines when writing.
10. Produce approximately his last name.

Poor Spatial Orientation

Understanding of spatial concepts such as *up, down, top* and *bottom* are important for correct letter formation and spacing of words. Many learning disabled children have a poor sense of directionality and confuse the strokes when writing. They are unable to follow when the teacher says, "Go below the red line" or "Circle to the left."

Inability to Copy Shapes

The ability to copy shapes correctly is required for a child to write fluently. Jordan (1977) points out that a frequent mistake children make is to draw "ears" at the corner of circles, squares or triangles. Other children add or omit an extra stroke, or copy from right to left. Errors such as these indicate that a child may have writing difficulties when presented with words.

Other Reasons

Orton (1937) suggested three possible reasons for writing difficulties. First, if a child is forced to use his nondominant hand (that is, he is made to write with his right hand when he prefers using his left), it may affect the legibility of his writing. The child may complain of feeling tired, or find even a simple task like copying very demanding. Second, there may be a delay in hand dominance. When there is a delay in establishing hand preference, the child may not acquire adequate visual memory of the graphic symbols or motor movements required for writing (apraxia). A third reason for illegible writing is incorrect slant of the paper. For right-handed persons the base of the paper should be angled to the right. For left-handed persons it should be slanted to the left (see Figure 6.1).

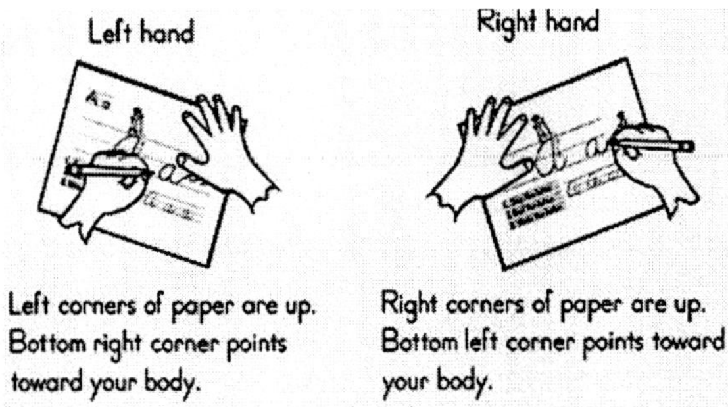

Figure 6.1: A Sketch to show the Corresponding Positions of the Paper and Hand for Left – and Right-Handed Writers

**Source:* S.T. Orton Reading, Writing and Speech Problems in Children. New York, W.W. Norton & Company Inc. 1964, p.182. Reprinted by permission of the Orton Dyslexia Society, Baltimore Md.

Kaminsky and Powers (1981, p. 21) identified five problems that may lead to poor writing:

1. Disorders of visual perception – the inability to recall how a letter looks
2. Failure to integrate the visual image of a letter with the correct motor response.
3. Poor efficiency and control of the intrinsic muscles in the hand.
4. Faulty motor memory related to the storage of motor information in the brain.
5. Difficulty in perceiving the spatial requirements of a task.

Manuscript or Cursive Writing?

An old debate that continues to persist is which kind of writing should be taught first – manuscript or cursive? Recent research suggests that handwriting problems could be reduced if cursive writing is taught before manuscript (Banas and Wills, 1970; McGinnis, 1963; Strauss and Lehtinen, 1947). These researchers claim that teaching cursive writing first, helps to increase fluency of movement, reduces reversals, and improves spacing between words. It also eliminates the need to later learn a "second" style of writing. This view is contested by Johnson and Myklebust (1967). They suggest that manuscript letters are easier to learn because of the fewer movements required and the appearance of the letters is consistent. Wallace and Kauffman (1978, p.204) also observe that "cursive writing should not be taught to children who are still experiencing difficulties with manuscript writing. In all likelihood, children who experience extreme difficulties with manuscript will also experience failure with cursive writing."

The decision whether or not to teach cursive handwriting first is preferably left to the teacher who can judge for herself the abilities of the individual child. However, one teaching strategy that should help is to constantly point out the similarity between the two kinds of writing. Problems arise if the child thinks of cursive writing as an entirely new writing system and cannot connect it with the manuscript letters. This is where the teacher comes in. She has to constantly reinforce the association between the printed and the cursive word. Cursive writing also requires very complex motor movements and fine motor coordination, which many learning-disabled children lack. It is best therefore to teach one form for both reading and writing rather than try to switch between the two forms.

In their study, Lewis and Lewis (1965) found that first-grade children made the following handwriting errors in order of frequency:

1. The five most difficult letters (incorrect size) were the descenders: *q*, *g*, *p*, *y* and *j*.
2. The letters *n*, *d*, *q*, and *y* were frequently written wrong.

3. The letter *m* was the most difficult of the nondescending letters.
4. Incorrect relationship of letter parts was greater in letters *k, R, M,* and *m* than in any other letter.
5. The most frequent error in the letter *U* was incorrect relationship of parts (partial omission).
6. The inversion error occurred in the letter *G.*
7. The easiest letters were *l, o, L, O* and *H.*
8. Errors in the letter *a* were mainly due to incorrect size and relationship of the large arc to the vertical line.
9. Boys were more prone to errors than girls.
10. The next ten most difficult letters were: *R, D, Y, u, M, S, b, e, r, and Z.*

Assessment of Handwriting Disorders

Formal Assessment

Most standardized tests have a handwriting component. For example, the Woodcock Johnson Tests of Achievement has a handwriting sample assessment. The Test of Written Language (TOWL-3) has a very comprehensive analysis of all the components of written language, including handwriting. These tests eliminate the subjective element in scoring and are easy to administer.

Informal Assessment

Informal assessments can be used by teachers and parents to determine a handwriting disorder. The process is simple. Collect handwriting samples using a series of structured tasks. Towle (1978) suggests asking the students to copy the sentence "The quick brown fox jumps over the lazy dog" from the board (1) five times using their normal handwriting, (2) three times using their best handwriting, and (3) as many times as possible in a three-minute period. This sample should then be analyzed, using a checklist such as the one provided by Kampinsky and Powers (1981, pp. 21–22).

It is also important to observe the manner in which the student actually writes. What hand does he prefer? How many times does he look between the board and the paper? Does he voice the words as he writes? A simple instruction from the teacher such as "Write the alphabet" will indicate many underlying problems. Some times a mixture of upper case and lower-case letters will be used; or, the student may alternate between cursive and manuscript letters. Reversals may also be observed. Assessment should help in distinguishing whether the problem is one of visual perception, memory, or motor coordination. Ask the student to copy any wrong formations three times each (three trials help to establish error consistency). If the child is able to copy correctly from the given model, the problem is possibly one of visual memory, that is, he cannot remember the shape of the letter. If he continues to make mistakes, a problem with visual perception or visual-motor coordination may be suspected. However, as with reading disabilities, there is a great deal of overlap between the two areas of visual memory and visual perception and further referral to an Occupational Therapist may be required for a definitive diagnosis.

Kaminsky and Powers (1981, pp. 21–22) provide a list of specific characteristics that help determine a handwriting disorder:

Kan – can	bol (ball)	fo (from)
Ded – bed	pet (pit)	den (done)
cot (sat)	tuc (cut)	eit (eat)
sun (sit)	dook (book)	mom (more)
cm (come)	sum (some)	pla (play)

find a way to gat ther (Find a way to get there)
come you're her (Comb your hair)

Instructional Methods for Teaching Handwriting

There are many different approaches to remedying handwriting disorders. One approach suggests improving the underlying visual-motor processes. A second method focuses directly on producing correctly formed letters and words. A third approach emphasizes the use of prompts and cues, and multi-sensory stimulation. Many commercial programmes are available to teach handwriting, and as always, selection should be determined by student needs.

Reversals when writing is a frequently occurring problem. The most effective strategies to correct reversals are offered by kinesthetic and multisensory programs. The Magic Ruler (Kirschner) is a wonderful tool for correction of reversals; it is easy to use and can be ordered from www.healthyplace.com.

Orton recommended kinesthetic training to first establish motor movements. The student had to close his eyes when writing so that he could attend to the motor patterns and not use vision. Strokes should be practiced on the palm of the hand to give kinesthetic feedback to the learner. Verbal rehearsal strategies are also helpful. The child should be encouraged to verbalize the movements as he writes. For example, reversals of d and b are overcome by verbal rehearsal of "c comes before d" (that is, c|). Using a transparent overlay containing the model letters will allow the learner to self-check his writing.

Computers vs Handwriting

If no improvement occurs even after several years of intervention, it is best to switch to alternative modes for written communication such as a computer. As children enter the higher grades, class tests, note taking, and writing of reports may become very laborious activities. The computer offers the best avenue for improved writing. Several software programs (see Appendix 2) are available for children of all ages, which teach keyboarding skills such as the Type to Learn program (www.k12software.com). The Alpha Smart is a simple, portable, computer that may be used with children in the elementary and upper elementary grades in the classroom (www.alphasmart.com).

Technological tools can make the process of writing easier as well as more motivating for students with a learning diability. Word processing, for example, provides at least three possible advantages for these students: (1) revising can be done without tedious recopying, (2) the resulting paper looks neater and presents well, and (3) typing provides an inherently easier means for producing text when fine motor difficulties are present (MacArthur, 1999). Technological tools can also provide support for planning and revising through the use of outlining and semantic mapping software, multimedia applications, and prompting programs. In addition, they allow the use of spell checkers, grammar and style checkers, and speech synthesis programs. Finally, the use of computer networks allows children to collaborate and communicate easily with audiences that extend beyond their classroom.

Unfortunately, not all learning-disabled students take easily to keyboarding and other technological tools. Many find it very difficult to locate the letters on the keyboard and feel frustrated at their slow speed. Similarly, a spell checker will not eliminate spelling errors or the need for spelling instruction, as students with a learning disability only correct about one-half of their errors when using such devices (MacArthur, Graham, Haynes, & De La Paz, 1996). Word processing is not the magic bullet that many have hoped it would be. Some studies show increased text length and quality when students use the word processor compared to handwriting, and others show the opposite pattern. What studies have not empirically examined is the degree to which students are fluent and automatic in typing effects the writing. Apel (2002) suggests that when young learning-disabled students are taught to rely only on keyboarding instead of using a pencil, it slows down their ability to acquire mental orthographic representation, and this may affect spelling and reading.

Clearly, for technological tools to be effective, students must also develop the knowledge, skill, will, and self-regulation so critical to effective writing. A computer is not a substitute for good teaching but can take the stress out of writing and result in better quality writing samples.

Disorders of Spelling

A spelling disability tends to co-exist with a reading disability and with a handwriting disability. Interest in spelling disorders has revived over the past twenty-five years or so. Experts have been investigating the connection between spelling disorders and oral language and reading. Compared to the research on reading, though, much less work has been done in the areas of spelling.

Karan's Story

Karan Nanda is now in the fourth grade but has always hated spellings. He starts to doodle and scribble all over his notebook the moment the teacher starts dictation. He says he feels confused looking at the letters "jumping around." His teacher says she has caught him many times trying to cheat from his neighbour's book. His mother wakes him up very early on the morning of his English tests to revise the spelling words but he still gets them wrong. Mrs. Nanda has tried many different methods. Sometimes, she makes Karan write each word five times. "When I make him sound out each letter it confuses him even more so now I just have him mug up the words by heart. When we have holidays, I let him type on the computer and use the spell check to correct his spellings. He loves that." His errors clearly indicate the kinds of errors commonly found in the spellings of learning disabled students – letter reversals (*b* for *d*), reversals of whole words (*tuc* for *cut*), confused sounds /c/ with /s/ (*sat* as *cot*), phonetic spellings of nonphonetic words (*some* as *sum*), and so on.

Understanding Spellings

Spelling is a complex, language-based skill. Many people make the mistake of thinking that spelling is a visual-spatial skill but this is not completely true. Spelling is based on several linguistic components such as *phonology*, *orthography*, *semantics*, and *morphology*.

Phonological awareness is the ability to identify and manipulate the sound structures of language. It is a strong predictor of early childhood spelling abilities (Ehri, 2000; Nation and Hulme, 1997).

Orthographic knowledge is understanding how to translate spoken language into written form. For example, the sound /k/ can be represented by the letters *k, c, cc, ch*, or *qu*. It also includes knowledge of rules for acceptable sounds. For example, English speakers should know that the *qd* combination does not exist in the English language. And, certain sound patterns are impossible, for example the digraph *ck* never appears in a word in the *initial* position but can be found at the end of a word. Cassar and Treiman (2004, pg 629) clearly explain that: "Orthographic knowledge also includes an understanding of the conventions of the writing system, including knowledge about spaces between words, acceptable and unacceptable letter sequences, and the various representations for certain phonemes, depending on such factors as their position in a word. This knowledge, in addition to phonology, then influences spelling."

Semantics refers to the use of vocabulary knowledge to spell words. Students who do not use their semantic knowledge are likely to confuse the spellings of homophones. Homophones are words that sound alike but have different meanings and spellings, such as *witch, which*; *their, there*; *fair, fare*. A student can store and retrieve spellings for homophones only when he understands their meaning.

Morphological awareness refers to the awareness of morphemes, the smallest units of language that carry meaning (prefixes, suffixes, rots and base words). This awareness helps the speller recognize certain spelling rules. For example, use of the past tense *ed* (beg becomes *begged*). Morphological awareness helps the speller understand the relationship between base words and derived words. For example, *busy* and *business*; *play* and *playing*; *vis* and *visual* or *vision*. It increases the child's comprehension as he reads.

Spelling is closely interlinked with reading in development. Both are linguistic skills and follow a similar course of acquisition and rely on phonological and morphological awareness, orthographic and semantic knowledge. Interestingly, researchers have found that learning to spell increases reading abilities (Apel and Masterson, 2001; Kelman and Apel, in press).

Theories of Spelling Development

Researchers have suggested different theories of spelling development. A full analysis of these theories is beyond the scope of this book but some key approaches are discussed here.

According to ***the stage theory of development*** (Bear, Invernizzi, Templeton, and Johnston, 2000), some types of information are used at one stage but not at another. In the first or *prephonetic* stage, children spell by scribbling. Little attention is paid to the relationship between sounds and letters; or, to the specific letter shapes. They rely mostly on visual clues. As children acquire names of letters, they try to write the sounds they hear. In this second or *semiphonetic* stage, they often use one letter for the whole word based on how the name of that letter sounds rather than the sound the letter creates. In the third or *phonetic* stage, children rely on their phoneme-grapheme correspondences as they spell. In the fourth stage, *within-word stage*, children can demonstrate an understanding of the orthographic rules such as marking long vowels with two vowel letters.

According to stage theory, children begin to rely on their understanding of morphology much later, around the third or fourth grades.

Recently, stage theory has been questioned by researchers who put forth ***the repertoire theory of spelling development.*** Experts point out (Bourassa and Treiman, 2001; Kelman and Apel, in press) that children use linguistic skills *throughout* the process of learning to spell. Children use multiple strategies and a variety of linguistic knowledge (phonologic, orthographic, semantic, morphologic) as they develop their spelling abilities.

Phonological awareness is a critical foundation for spelling, as it is in reading. Many studies (Muter, Hulme, Snowling and Taylor, 1998) have shown that children must possess some phonological skill in order to grasp the alphabetical principle.

Ehri (1997) discussed processes by which words may be spelled – *by memory, by analogy, or by invention.* Spelling a word by memory can occur only if the child already knows the word. Spelling a word by analogy requires the child to recognize the phonological similarity between the new word and other known words. Spelling by invention requires that the speller should break up words into phonemes and apply alphabetical knowledge of phoneme-grapheme correspondence to create spellings. Young children have little knowledge of spellings and rely on invention. Many studies have demonstrated a strong link between children's knowledge of letter names and spelling acquisition (Treiman and Kessler, 2003). Most children can identify a number of letters before they begin formal schooling. Letter-name knowledge helps children take their first steps towards understanding that writing is connected to speech. Children in kindergarten, first and second grade understand that writing represents the sounds in words. However, their spelling efforts are often inaccurate because their phonological skills are still at a basic level. They may spell *car* as *cr*, *hom* for *home*, *bot* for *boat*. Errors such as these become less common as the child begins to develop orthographic knowledge.

As a child is exposed to printed words, his orthographic and morphological knowledge begins to influence his use of spellings. If phonological skill is poor, then improvement may be very slow. Studies have shown that individuals with dyslexia rely heavily on orthographic knowledge to support their spellings.

The development of phonological skills and orthographic information are co-dependent. Each supports and interacts with the other. (Ehri, 1997; Perfetti, 1992, 1997). Children with dyslexia have weak phonological skills whereas their orthographic skills are adequate. This imbalance in skill retards the progress of dyslexic children in both reading and spelling. It may be possible to bridge the gap by explicitly teaching dyslexic children to break spellings apart and to break pronunciations apart. Children with dyslexia should benefit from the explicit pairing of visual and verbal word components.

Assessment of Spelling Disorders

Formal Assessment

Several formal tests have a subsection to assess spelling such as:

- The Wide Range Achievement Test (WRAT, Jastak and Jastak, 1978)
- Peabody Individual Achievement Test (PIAT, Dunn and Markwardt, 1970)
- Test of Written Language (TOWL, Larsen and Hammill, 1976)
- Woodcock Johnson Tests of Achievement–IV (WJ-IV, Mather and Woodcock, 2001)

It is important to choose a test that is appropriate for the specific deficit. For example, on the WRAT and the TOWL, the student is asked to write words and use them in sentences, a task that entails complete recall. But on the PIAT he has to only recognize and select the correct spelling. So the teacher must be very clear as to which skill is being assessed in a particular test. Scores from the spelling tests should be compared to general intellectual ability or to reading performance to ascertain any other areas that may be contributing to this deficit.

Informal Assessments

Teacher made spelling tests can be just as effective as formal assessments. Houck (1984) suggested that the following questions could help guide an informal spelling assessment:

- What kinds of spelling errors are made during dictation or spontaneous writing?
- What kinds of errors occur when the student is asked to spell known words versus unfamiliar words?

- Can the learner identify his own errors or errors presented in some other written piece?
- When errors are located, can he correct them independently?
- Can he identify the correct spelling in a dictionary or other learning material?
- Does his difficulty with spelling interfere with his motivation to write?
- Does he use strategies to study new words?
- Does he know and use spelling rules?
- Can he divide a word into syllables (do "word-sums," for example, relate = re + late)?

These questions will further assist in making a comprehensive intervention plan for the learner.

Instructional Methods for Teaching Spelling

A spelling disorder never goes away by itself. One definitive conclusion from recent research (McIntyre, 1995) is that students with spelling disorders need *explicit instruction* in spelling. Students with a learning disability tend to need more individualized, intensive training in these skills than other students for gains to be noticed (O' Connor *et al.*, 1996). Several researchers have demonstrated the benefits of direct instruction in phonological processing for reading and spelling (Rubin and Eberhardt, 1996). However, the gaps between spelling and reading skills may widen over time (Moats, 1995). Torgesen and colleagues (2001) recently reported an intervention study of 60 children with severe reading disabilities. Subjects received two individual, 50-minute sessions per day for 8 weeks in phonemic awareness and phonemic decoding skills. Whereas significant gains were reported in word recognition and reading comprehension, spelling skills improved to a lesser extent and generally were not maintained over time.

Which Instructional Practices Work Best?

McNaughton, Hughes, and Clark (1994) reviewed 27 published studies on spelling instruction for students with learning disability.

They identified several instructional practices to be particularly effective, including the following:

- Limit the number of new words introduced daily.
- Include peer-assisted and student-directed instruction.
- Instruct students to name letters aloud as they practice spelling.
- Incorporate instruction in morphemic analysis.
- Provide immediate error imitation and correction.
- Provide periodic review and retesting.

Scott (2000) emphasized that four types of spelling activities are supported by research: memorizing words, word analysis and sorting, authentic reading and writing activities, and instruction in the strategic self-monitoring of spelling.

It goes without saying that good spelling instruction should be targeted at the students' level of emerging skills. Teachers generally use weekly spelling lists based on words that appear frequently in the textbook. These lists may not be developmentally appropriate for the learning disabled student as many errors persist well into middle school. Kamhi and Linton (2000) noted that poor spellers might follow a different developmental pattern as they try to spell, often relying excessively on visual memory due to innate deficits in phonological processing.

Developmental Stages of Spelling Instruction

Teach Basic Phoneme-Grapheme Correspondence and Orthographic Patterns.

The first task is for the young child to master the basic alphabetic system. Children are usually able to sort out for themselves the simplest of phoneme-grapheme correspondences and can match up some sounds with their letter names (for example, *can-d* for *candy*). This is the beginning of *invented spelling*. Here is a written sample of invented spelling done by Sumita, a five year old kindergartener:

Th mn wnt hm (The man went home)
I lik to pla boll (I like to play ball)

Invented spelling may not look like any real spelling words, but it helps the child to acquire spelling knowledge. However, the difficulty with learning disabled students is, because they have phonological processing deficits, direct instruction in these skills is required for them to spell. The child will need instruction in how to articulate each phoneme, using for example, manipulatives or blocks to represent each phoneme. She may need practice in hearing, saying, counting and comparing phonemes within words. The Lindamood (1998) program is one example of a structured spelling program that works well. Bear *et al.* (2000) and Moats (1995) provide explicit scope and sequence charts for teaching spelling.

Formal spelling instruction generally should begin with the introduction of a few consonants and short vowels, along with a few high frequency sight words. The first consonants should be the ones closest to their sounds, such as b, p, t, s. The sounds h, w, and y should be later. Ready lists of words can be found in:

- *Words Their Way* (Bear *et al.*, 2000)
- *Spellmaster* Greenbaum (1987)
- *Teaching spelling* by Henderson (1990).

Paradoxically, research says that its important to introduce some words that are less predictable as this helps the student to look out for spelling patterns and to identify words that are different. Consonant blends, digraphs and double-vowel patterns are especially difficult for learning-disabled students and may require extra practice.

When teaching specific spelling patterns, teachers should incorporate a variety of activities that are linked with phonological awareness, reading, and vocabulary building activities. Multi-sensory strategies, such as used in the Orton Gillingham and Fernald programs, are sound. More recent programs are Graham and Freeman's Five-step Study Strategy (1986) and Berninger, Abbott, *et al.'s* Eight-Step Method (1998). The basic procedure outlined in these methods is to see the word, say it, write or trace it, and check if it's correct. Students with a learning disability may need to use multi-sensory approaches for longer periods of time than other students.

Word-sorting Activities

Word-sorting activities should be introduced early on in spelling instruction and can be used for children of all ages. For younger children, the teacher writes individual words on cards and has them sort the cards into categories such as *ar* words or *or* words. This type of activity encourages mental processing and retention by encouraging students to look for patterns across words. Scott (2000) has a list of words that can be sorted out. The physical act of categorizing facilitates learning, even in older learning-disabled students.

Teaching Individual Words

Students with learning disability find it very hard to recall the correct spelling of high-frequency sight words and may require up to 40 opportunities to spell a word before they get it right. One reason for this is that words such as *of, for* lack concrete meaning and serve a grammatical function. They depend on a contextual sentence for meaning. Another reason is that high-frequency words are sometimes homophones (there/their; here/hear) and require an understanding of their meaning, along with spelling recall. Such words require explicit instruction, using a multi-sensory approach.

Research has demonstrated that for poor spellers, the number of spelling words to be learned must be no more than three to five words per day, or six to twelve new words per week (Moats, 1995; Graham and Voth, 1990).

Teaching Spellings to Older Students

Older children show major deficiencies because words have increased in complexity; spelling instruction is no longer taught to them explicitly; and deficits in phonological processing persist. Teachers need to be flexible and innovative. Methods that did not work when the student was younger may now be easier for the older student to grasp. Very few schools continue to provide explicit spelling instruction after say grades 7 or 8 but learning disabled students need a lot more practice with spellings. The teacher can keep their interest alive by making lesson plans that incorporate vocabulary, reading, and spellings. Some excellent materials for older students use syllable patterns such as *Megawords* (by Johnson & Bayrd, 1983) and *Syllable Plus* (by Stoner, 1985).

Older students can also be taught to examine distinctive features of the word such as word endings, prefixes and suffixes. This is called structural analysis. Dictate the base word first and the student can write the suffix. Review rules taught in second and third grade such as "words which end in *y* need to change to an *i* before adding a suffix." Masterson and Scott (1997) recommend that there should be some spelling activity in every lesson for older students. For example, students can be asked to find a particular spelling pattern in a chapter; or, write a story using specific word patterns. Older, bright learning-disabled students can enjoy deriving the origins of words. The challenge of word derivatives can be intellectually stimulating for older dyslexic student. Moats (1995) and Henry (1988) provide detailed lesson plans for spelling units for older students. There are many ways to encourage students to correct their own spelling mistakes (Graham, 1999; Berninger, Abbott *et al.*, 1998):

- Locate the specific letter or part of the word where the error has occurred.
- Use peers to help in editing.
- Use a spell check program on the computer.

Spelling difficulties are very persistent and stay with the individuals into adulthood. Both students and teachers experience a lot of frustration and a sense of failure when progress slows down. Perhaps our most important goal as educators should be to help learning disabled students with enough practice and knowledge of spelling rules that they feel confident of trying out new words when writing. Spelling should be placed in the larger context of student learning. Learning disabled students become so restricted when they write that it is difficult to access the richness of their ideas and thoughts. The goal of instruction should be to encourage writing as a form of communication using materials that contribute to the child as a global learner.

Key Principles of Spelling Instruction

- Familiarize yourself with basic linguistic terms, rules and patterns that relate to English spelling.
- Provide direct instruction in phonological awareness skills.
- Group words according to spelling patterns, and give as many examples of each spelling pattern as you can.
- Teach a single spelling rule at a time, and apply that rule to words. Also demonstrate where the rule does not apply.
- Choose spelling lists carefully. Words must correspond with words that occur in the child's reader. Do not choose words the student cannot read.
- Do not hesitate to use simple methods like colour coding, underlining, and increasing the font size. Or, highlight the letters that differ in a pair of homophones (e.g. their/there)
- Begin with spelling of words that have the most structure (one spelling pattern), and then move on to words with less structure.
- Use word sorting and word building activities.
- Introduce a few sight words daily and give lots of practice. Research shows that regardless of the number of words provided, between seven and eight words were learned over a three-day period. (Bryant *et al.* 1981, p.203).
- Use multi-sensory techniques and mnemonic devices (you *hear* with your *ear).*
- Give immediate feedback whether a spelling is correct or incorrect.
- Practice changing word forms in structured activities. For example: *Sue is related to John. John and Sue are relatives.*
- Give sentence dictation using specific word patterns.
- Over learning is desirable.

Written Expression

The content of written language is an important aspect of communication. Learning-disabled children often produce compositions that are immature, and poorly organized even though they may have bright ideas and a vivid imagination. Interestingly, learning-disabled students tend to produce an "oral" style of writing, that is, they write as if they are in casual conversation with a friend. Their writing pieces contain slang words such as 'Hey'; 'OK' or 'What's up, man?' Also, because they read less, their access to factual knowledge is limited, and they have much less to write about. For some, the effort of putting their ideas down on paper is so great that it leaves them unable to take care of the other aspects of writing such as organizing, planning and stylistic details. Singer and Bashir (2004), summarized the research on learning disabled students as following:

They have difficulty reading their assignments and knowing how to complete their work. They struggle with planning, organizing, and revising their writing. Their use of language is problematic in terms of syntax, vocabulary, and they make frequent errors in spelling and writing mechanics. They have difficulty making transitions from one step in writing to the next. They often appear to have difficulty allocating sufficient cognitive resources to meet various writing demands (i.e. knowing where to begin, how to stay on task and develop a topic, etc.) As a result they are ineffective and inefficient writers.

Writing demands skills of planning, organizing, generating, and revising. Students with learning disability fail to use explicit planning and organizational strategies. In a study done by MacArthur and Graham (1999), students with learning disabled averaged less than 1 minute of time planning prior to writing, unless they are taught explicitly how to plan. Even when they have been taught to brainstorm, learning-disabled students produce written work that is poorly organized and incoherent. Revising their work too is hard for them. When asked to revise they tend to focus on spellings, capitalization, and punctuation errors. They seldom examine finer aspects of writing such as improving a word, sentence or introducing new ideas.

Learning disabled students may have slow processing speed, which affects their performance on verbal memory tasks. They are often at a loss for words. This occurs partly because they lack sufficient knowledge of academic content, and partly because they struggle to retain the vocabulary found in content subjects. Here we see the effects of oral language and reading difficulties on knowledge acquisition. Students who avoid reading have less exposure to textual knowledge. Having little to say, they don't write much.

Many learning disabled students do not have large working memory capacity and either forget what they wanted to say or are unable to attend to other aspects of writing (spelling, punctuation etc.). In order to access words and ideas, and hold them in one's mind long enough to get them written down, a strong working memory is required. Working memory is the buffer between long-term storage and generating text in writing.

Many experts suggest that learning disabled students should be allowed to use a computer or dictate their ideas to an adult who can write for them. These alternative writing methods may not work, and may create additional problems. For one thing, dictating ideas may be hard for the learning disabled student who struggles with language and/or working memory. A student who has difficulty finding the right words may dictate a paragraph that is disorganized, poorly formed and incoherent. Another difficulty could arise when dictating the text to an adult writer or scribe. Because of the problems many learning disabled students have with memory, they may forget what they have dictated or recall what they are planning to say.

The fact remains that a child who is deficient in oral language skills will also lack in written expression. Expression of ideas is a major source of difficulty for learning disabled students. Many researchers have suggested there is a very strong relationship between oral language ability and experiences and the quality of written language. The child must be given adequate experiences to write about, and receive exposure to situations, which will provoke him into questioning, debate, thinking, and arguments.

Assessment of Written Expression

Formal Assessments

The Test of Written Language (TOWL-3) and the Writing Assessment Program (WRAP) are two good examples of standardized assessments that examine many components of written language. The TOWL asks the student to write a story based on a given picture. A scoring rubric is provided for the tester.

The Writing Assessment Program (WRAP, by ERB) provides a direct measure of writing ability by asking for a writing sample from each student, using a verbal prompt. For example, "My school is the best school in the world because..." The piece of writing is then evaluated using a rubric that examines elements such as knowledge of grammar and writing conventions, word choice, how well the student can think, plan, and use language to convey meaning.

Informal Assessments

Informal assessments can be teacher-made. A sample of the student's written work is collected and analyzed, using checklists or writing rubrics. Writing skills in a variety of areas must be assessed. For example, select a piece of spontaneous writing on a topic chosen by the student; and, a factual paragraph that allows one to assess the student's note-taking and outlining skills. Try to determine if the errors exhibit some kind of pattern. A statement of specific objectives, keeping in view the student's age, strengths, and weaknesses, must follow the assessment. For each objective, define the method that will be used for remedying the deficit. Strategies must be consistent with the student's learning styles, and be transferable across different subjects. The instructional objectives should be revised as the child meets the targets specified.

Instructional Methods for Teaching Written Expression

When improving written expression, the initial emphasis should be on enriching the quality of the child's experiences. The child should be taught to look at writing not as just another academic task but as a way of self-expression and communication. Writing should emerge from the student's thoughts and interests rather than be viewed as a mechanical task where rules of grammar need to be followed. Gleason (1982) suggested that writing could be taught in three stages: (1) the prewriting or reflective period where time is given to mentally thinking about a topic, (2) the writing stage, and (3) the editing or revising stage. He observed that students are asked to write about a topic but not much time is given to them to think about that topic. Experts have suggested that as much as 85% of one's time should be spent in the prewriting stage, 1 % in the actual writing and 14% in revising it (Murray, 1976, p. 80). An interesting step-by-step procedure is outlined by Gleason (1982, p. 575) as preparation for getting students to write:

1. Show an object to the student and ask him to describe all the varied aspects of that object. Record his ideas on a large backboard or chart.
2. Group the details in categories of appearance, use, even colour coding the points.
3. The ideas should then be ordered in the sequence in which they will be written.
4. Let the student write out the first draft with teacher assistance.
5. Type the first draft for the student, making basic corrections in grammar and spelling since the focus here is on organization of ideas and not spellings.
6. Ask the student to make other corrections. Retype the second draft.

In this manner the teacher actually walks the students through all the steps of composition rather than "discussing" the main argument with the class (which is what is done in most schools) and leaving the student to organize his thoughts independently. With children from rich experiential backgrounds, writing should be introduced as a structured, concrete task. Paragraph writing is a skill that needs to be developed step by step in students. Show the students how to analyze passages from magazines, newspapers or books, using short paragraphs, with clear concise ideas. Make them underline the main topic and idea of that passage and delete what is irrelevant or extraneous. Discuss why paragraphs are needed and why "transitions" are required as we move from one paragraph to another. Students should be encouraged to keep a diary, write articles for the newspaper, react to local events, and write letters and short stories. In all these writing activities, the students should check if they have maintained the logical flow of ideas within paragraphs, used the appropriate indentation, avoided redundancy, and maintained the same tone throughout (formal, informal, friendly, and so on).

Help students understand that writing is a form of communication. What they write should make sense to the reader. They may need specific help with focusing on unclear sentences and rewriting them. Sometimes a teacher may have to say, "I can't look inside your head and tell what you are thinking. So please write clearly so that I can understand what you are trying to say." Organize the classroom for large-group, small-group, and independent activities. One way to do this is to establish centres within a classroom: the Listening Centre is where the student listens to recordings of source materials relevant to their writing. At the Viewing Centre, they can look at videos films to get ideas for their topic. At the Conference Centre, they can talk with their peers. At the Computer Centre, they can use the Internet as another source of information. At the Writing Centre, children write on a variety of topics. They can discuss with each other their choice of words, spelling, and stylistic issues. At the Resource Centre, they can look at books, magazines, and so on. At the Teacher Centre, the teacher can work on a small group for individual instruction. Then she sends them back to another centre, and works with the next group. Students are given a weekly plan so they know how to rotate between the Centres.

Strategies for Writing

- Learning disabled students tend to have difficulty with working memory, and would benefit from the use of audio recorders to store information. Or, provide a planning sheet and have them refer to that as they write.
- Teach students that different kinds of genres (mysteries, horror stories, action adventures, etc.) require a different choice of words.
- Provide students with strategies for monitoring their own writing. Have them graph their own progress so they have visible record of their progress and of skills they still need to work on.
- Do not expect computers alone to transform learning disabled students who are poor writers into good writers.
- Be patient and do not expect instant mastery of writing skills. Becoming a good writer takes time and evolves over a long period.

References

Apel, K. (2002, March). Spelling it out for SLP's: Spelling development, assessment and intervention. Paper presented at the California meeting of the Speech-Language-Hearing Association, Los Angeles.

Banas, N. & Wills, I.H. (1970). The vulnerable child and cursive writing. In John Arena (ed.) *Building Handwriting Skills in Dyslexic Children,* pp. 23–25. San Rafael, Calif.

Bear, D., Invernizzi, M. Templeton, S. & Johnston, F. (2000). Words their way: Word study for phonics, vocabulary and spelling instruction (2nd ed.). Upper Saddle River, NJ: Prentice-Hall.

Berninger, V., Abbot, R., Rogan, L., Reed, E., Abott, S., Brooks, A., *et al.* (1998). Teaching spelling to children with specific learning disabilities: The mind's ear and eye beat the computer or pencil. *Learning Disability Quarterly, 21,* 106–122.

Brueckner, L.S. & Bond, G.L. (1955). *The diagnosis and treatment of learning difficulties.* New York: Appleton-Century-Crofts.

Bryant, N.D., Drabin, I.R. & Gettinger, M. (1981, 200–03). Effects of varying unit size on spelling achievement in learning disabled children. *Journal of Learning Disabilities,* 14, 4.

Bourassa, D.C. & Treiman, R. (2001). Spelling development and disability: The importance of linguistic factors. *Language, Speech and Hearing Services in Schools*, 32, 172–181.

Dunn, L. & Markwadt, F.C. (1970). Peabody Individual Achievement test. Circle Pines, Minn.: American Guidance Service.

Gillingham, A. & Stillman, B.W. (1973). Remedial Training for Children with Specific Disability in *Reading, Spelling, and Penmanship* (7th ed.). Cambridge, Mass.: Educators Publishing Service, Inc.

Ehri, L.C. (2000). Learning to read and learning to spell: Two sides of a coin. *Topics in Language Disorders*, 20(3), 19–36.

Gould, B.W. (2001). Curricular strategies for written expression. In A.M. Bain, L.L. Bailet & L.C. Moats (Eds.), *Written language disorders: Theory into practice* (2nd ed., pp. 185–220). Austin, TX: PRO-ED.

Graham, S. (1999). Handwriting and spelling instruction for students with learning disabilities: A review. *Learning Disability Quarterly*, 22, 78–98.

Graham, S. & Voth, V. (1990). Spelling instruction: Making modifications for students with learning disabilities. *Academic Therapy, 25*, 447–457.

Gleason, *Writing a way out of the learning disabled dilemma.* Academic Therapy, 17, 5, 1982, 573–579.

Goodman, L. & Hammill, D.D. (1975). *The Basic School Inventory.* Chicago: Follett.

Hammill, D. & Larsen, S. (1978). Test of Written Language. Austin, Tex.: Pro-Ed.

Henderson, E. (1990). *Teaching spelling.* Boston: Houghton Mifflin.

Henry, M.K. (1988). Beyond phonics: Integrated decoding and spelling instruction based on word origin and structure. *Annals of Dyslexia, 38*, 258–275.

Houck, Cherry K. (1984). *Learning Disabilities: Understanding Concepts, Characteristics and Issues.* Prentice-Hall, Inc. Englewood Cliffs, New Jersey.

Jastak. J. & Jastak, S. (1978). Wide Range Achievement Test (rev. ed.). Wilmington, Del.: Jastak Associates.

Johnson, K. & Bayrd, P. (1983). *Megawords.* Cambridge, MA: Educators Publishing Services.

Johnson, D.J. & Myklebust, H.R. (1967). *Learning disabilities: Educational principles and practices.* New York: Grune & Stratton.

Jordan, D.R. (1977). *Dyslexia in the Classroom* (2nd. ed.). Columbus, Ohio: Charles E. Merrill Publishing Company.

Kaminsky, S. & Powers, R. (1981). Remediation of handwriting difficulties: A practical approach. *Academic Therapy, 17,* 1, 19–25.

Kamhi, A.G. & Hinton, L.N. (2000). Explaining individual differences in spelling ability. *Topics in Language Disorders, 20*(3), 37–49.

Kelman, M.K. & Appel, K. The effects of a multiple linguistic approach to spelling instruction: A case study. *Communication Disorders Quarterly.*

Lindamood, C.H. & Lindamood, P. (1998). *The Lindamood Phoneme Sequencing Program for reading, spelling and speech.* Austin, TX: PRO-ED.

MacArthur, C., Graham, S., Haynes, J. & De La Paz, S. (1996). Spelling checkers and students with learning disabilities. *Journal of Special Education, 30*, 35–57.

Masterson, J.J. & Scott, C. (1997). Improving spelling skills in children with and without language disorders. Seminar presented at the annual convention of the American Speech-Language-Hearing Association, Boston, MA.

McGinnis, A. (1963). *Aphasic Children.* Washington D.C.: Alexander Graham Bell Association for the Deaf., Inc.

McIntyre, E. (1995). Teaching and learning writing skills. *Journal of Reading Behavior, 27*, 213–242.

McNaughton, D., Hughes, C.A. & Clark, K. (1994). Spelling instruction for students with learning disabilities: Implications for research and practice. *Learning Disability Quarterly, 17,* 169–185.

Moats, L. (1995). *Spelling: Development, disability and instruction.* Baltimore: York Press.

Murray, D.M. (1976). Teach writing as a process not product. In R.L. Graves (ed.). *Rhetoric and Composition: A Sourcebook for Teachers,* pp. 80–82. Rochelle Park, N.J.: Hayden Book Company, Inc.

Nation, K. & Hulme, C. (1997). *Reading Research Quarterly,* 32, 154–167.

Orton, S. (1937). *Reading, writing, and speech problems in children.* New York: Norton.

O'Connor, R.E., *et al.* (1996). Ladders to Literacy. *Exceptional Children, 63*(1),117–130.

Perfetti, C.A. (1992). The repesentation problem in reading acquisition. In P.B. Gough *et al.* (eds.), *Reading acquisition* (pp. 145–174).Hillsadle, NJ: Erlbaum.

Perfetti, C.A. (1997). The psycholinguistics of spelling and reading. In C.A. perfetti *et al.* (Eds.), *Learning to spell: Research, theory and practice across languages* (pp.21–38). Mahwah, NJ: Erlbaum.

Ruben, H. & Eberhardt, N. (1996). Facilitating invented spelling. *Reading and Writing: An Interdisciplinary Journal,* 8, 27–43.

Scott, C.M. (2000). Principles and methods of spelling instruction: Applications for poor spellers. *Topics in Language Disorders, 20*(3), 66–82.

Stoner, J. (1985). *Syllable Plus.* Cambridge, MA: Educators Publishing Services.

Torgeson, J.K. *et al.* (2001). Intensive remedial instruction for children with severe reading disabilities. *Journal of Learning Disabilities, 34,* 33–58.

Towle, M. (1978). Assessment and remediation of handwriting deficits for children with learning disabilities (1978). *Journal of Learning Disabilities, 11,* 6, 43–50.

Wallace, G. & Kaufmann, J.M. (1978). *Teaching children with learning problems* (2nd. ed.). Columbus, Ohio: Charles E. Merrill.

Singer, B.D. & Bashir, A.S. (2004). EmPOWER: A strategy for teaching students with language learning disabilities how to write expository text. In E. Silliman and L. Wilkinson (Eds.), *Language and literacy learning,* New York: Guilford Press.

CHAPTER 7

Disorders of Mathematics: Dyscalculia

Harmeet's Story

Nine-year old Harmeet Singh has difficulty with arithmetic. She is now in Class 3 and still confuses the addition symbol + with the multiplication sign ×. She counts on her fingers, performs very poorly on mental math problems, and cannot tell the time accurately. Harmeet is highly distracted and inattentive. She forgets what steps she is using and often "borrows" twice from the same digit. Her concept of numbers over 300 is vague. The following is an extract from her worksheet to illustrate how she typically performs:

$$\begin{array}{r} 25 \\ +\ 36 \\ \hline 51 \end{array} \qquad \begin{array}{r} 19 \\ +\ 17 \\ \hline 12 \end{array} \qquad \begin{array}{r} 23 \\ -\ 13 \\ \hline 13 \end{array} \qquad \begin{array}{r} 70 \\ -\ 12 \\ \hline 62 \end{array}$$

Harmeet's mother, Mrs. Singh said, "It took Harmeet a long time to learn the days of the week and to write 1 to 100. She used to flip numbers around such as 6 with 9; 12 with 21; and 28 with 82. If she learns one concept, she forgets the previous one." Harmeet was diagnosed as having a specific learning disability in mathematics and is now receiving extra help in school. She is allowed to use a 'squares' notebook as this helps her align the numbers accurately. Her teacher is seriously considering permitting her to also use a calculator in class to increase her speed of processing. If nothing else, the calculator will help improve her self-confidence.

Introduction

Research in the analysis and remediation of problems related to mathematics has been rather neglected. Large numbers of school children continue to experience failure in this subject. Although the traditional term of *arithmetic* is now replaced by the all-inclusive "mathematics" under the influence of modern math programs, the nature of the difficulties remains the same. Children with arithmetic disabilities can be found at all age levels and early identification is very important.

Though it is not necessary that a dyslexic reader *must* demonstrate difficulties in arithmetic, certain deficits could occur across subjects. For example, difficulties in reading could affect the child's ability to solve word problems. Deficits that cause the child to invert or reverse words may spill over to numbers. Problems in visual discrimination may affect the child's ability to discriminate between numbers. Unlike reading, though, where the core deficit is a phonological deficit, nothing has been identified for mathematics, Mathematics is such a broad domain with so many sub disciplines that more than one variable may play a causal role. Sometimes the terms used – *mathematical difficulties*; *disabilities*; *dyscalculia*; *poor math achievement* could be quite confusing. Are these terms intended to be synonymous, exclusive or overlapping? The literature is not quite clear. Also, although mathematics consists of many other topics such as algebra, geometry, and measurement, most studies of young children with mathematical disability have mainly dealt with number work and arithmetic.

Findings from Research

Some consistent findings from mathematical disability research are discussed below. The recent surge in research has clearly established that mathematical disabilities are heterogeneous in nature. This is because arithmetic is not a single entity but is made up of many components – facts, ability to carry out procedures; understanding and use of arithmetical principles; estimation; word problems and so on. Dowker conducted a study in 1998 with children between the ages of 6 and 9. She found that arithmetic is not unitary and it is risky to assume that a child "does not understand maths" because he or she performs poorly in some calculation task. This study helps clarify why teachers are sometimes amazed how a child is able to memorize mathematical facts (multiplication tables) but cannot still carry out the procedures. Desoete, Roeyers, and De Clercq (2004) studied third grade Belgian students and found that children with and without mathematical disability can have strengths and weaknesses in almost any area of arithmetic.

It is indeed generally found that children with mathematical disability are more consistently weak in retrieving arithmetic facts from memory than at any other aspect of arithmetic. Several researchers confirm this finding (Jordan and Hanich, 2000). Children with mathematical disability rely on counting strategies when their peers are able to automatically retrieve facts (Miles, Haslum and Wheeler, 2001). In Dowker's study (in press) she found that 6 and 7 year olds with difficulty in mathematics could remember many number facts but they lacked strategies for working out sums. Bryant, Bryant, and Hammill (2000) carried out a large-scale study of 870 pupils with mathematical disability. They found that the commonest problem was a difficulty carrying out *multi-step* arithmetic problems.

Practice Breeds Confidence

A key researcher in the field of mathematical disability has been David Geary. Geary (2000) found that for many children, mathematical difficulties are not stable over time, and that some children outgrow their developmental delays. This is another reason why testing for mathematical difficulties must be done frequently as there can be a change between first and second grade.

Geary's research also indicates that students who struggled with mathematics in the elementary grades were unable to *automatically* retrieve arithmetic facts such as 4 + 3 = 7 or 9 × 8 = 72. Automaticity has been identified as an important skill that is required for the student to be able to attend to higher level reasoning processes (Geary, 2004; Hanish *et al.*, 2001). Longitudinal research shows that a third grader who cannot perform simple addition or subtraction goes on to struggle with more complicated concepts such as algebraic equations.

Another major finding is that students who have mathematical difficulties also have inefficient counting strategies (Jordan, 2003). Students poor in mathematic ability count on their fingers in second and third grades whereas their peers increasingly used verbal counting without fingers, which led them later to quickly do sophisticated mathematic manipulations. Siegler and Shrager (1984) studied the development of counting strategies in children and found that children use a variety of methods when counting and adding. For example, when figuring out the answer to 3 + 8, a child using an unsophisticated, inefficient strategy would first pick out 3 concrete objects and then 8 more objects, then count how many objects there are altogether. A more mature but still inefficient counting strategy is to begin at 3 and "count up" to 8. An even more mature approach would be to begin with the larger number 8 and count up 3, an approach that requires less counting. Some children will simply have this combination stored in memory and remember that it is 11.

Siegler's research reminds us that if a child can easily retrieve basic combinations (e.g. 6 + 6 = 12) then he can use this information to help quickly solve another problem.

Geary (1990) extended Siegler's research to mathematical disability by studying the counting strategy use of students with mathematical disability in the first grade. He discovered that students with mathematical disability depended on finger counting and made errors even when doing this. Maturity and efficiency of counting strategies are valid predictors of students' ability to profit from traditional mathematics instruction.

It is Important to Teach Efficient Counting Strategies

Recent research by Fuchs *et al.* (2004) has suggested that children with mathematical disability who are adequate readers show a different pattern of cognitive deficits than children with mathematical disability who are also poor readers. A distinguishing characteristic of this line of research involves the domains of mathematical cognition that are assessed. Much of the early research on children with mathematical disability was narrowly focussed, emphasizing only one area of computation. But more recently the research has focused on problem solving and number sense. Research also finds that abilities are uneven across areas of mathematics, especially among children with mathematical disability only.

Difficulties in reading seem to have a negative influence on children's development in general math achievement. In contrast, math abilities did not influence reading growth.

Another group of researchers have focussed on the concept of number sense (Bereiter and Scardamalia, 1981; Dehaene, 1997). Experts do not exactly agree about what number sense means but it includes flexibility when computing mentally, estimation, ability to see mathematical relationships and so on. Number sense allows students to think about mathematical problems and can be enhanced by formal or informal instruction before entering school. For example, in five and six year olds, the two components of number sense – counting and sense of quantity – are critical for proficient math problem.

Number Sense is Critical for Solving Problems

The Acquisition of Mathematical Concepts, According to Piaget

Piaget's stages of cognitive development correlate with the order in which children learn mathematical concepts. Object permanency, seriation, classification, conservation of quantity, one-to-one correspondence and evocative memory are some of the prerequisite concepts that emerge during the sensori-motor period (birth to two). However, these are not fully understood until the child enters the preoperational or concrete stage (age seven or eight years) and even then may need concrete manipulative aids. The child is able to deal with hypothetical thinking only at age eleven or twelve years, when he enters what Piaget called the *formal operational stage*. By this time, the child should:

- Understand basic spatial-temporal relationships and object permanency.
- Be able to take a perspective different from his own (decentration).
- Have sufficient perceptual skills to enable him to attend selectively to attributes (e.g. ignore colour and focus on the size of an object).
- Be able to conserve number and volume.
- Understand that events can be reversed, and
- Understand the relationship between time, speed and distance.

Causes of Dyscalculia

Sustained research in the area of why mathematical disabilities occur is sparse compared to the area of reading disabilities. As early as 1919, Henschen reported that "number blindness" could occur independently of specific reading disability. Later Cohn (1961) observed that memory and order disorders frequently occurred along with numerical problems. Cohn's study with forty neurologically injured adults focused specially on the multiplication process and led to the conclusion that:

1. Dyscalculia may result from lesions in widely disparate regions of the brain.
2. Lesions disturbing the physiology of the central visual apparatus profoundly alter the processes of arithmetical "order."

3. Where the lesions are present in regions other than the visual system, disturbed memory process primarily generate the arithmetical inaccuracies.

Soon after this, Luria (1980) suggested that spatial dysfunction is associated with the parieto-occipital regions of the brain (see Chapter 3), which results in numerical confusion (for example, 9 is seen as 6, 12 as 21) and an inability to discriminate notational signs and symbols (+, X, =). These types of problems were termed *primary arithmetical disturbance* or *primary acalculia.* Dysfunctions associated within the left temporal lobe were characterized by difficulties with complex operations involving a sequence of steps, or mental or oral calculation or reasoning. These disorders were termed *secondary arithmetical disturbance.*

Further research in these areas was conducted by Hacaen (1967) and Kosc (1974). Kosc (1974) introduced the term *developmental dyscalculia*, which he defined as "*a structural disorder of mathematics which has its origins as a genetic or constitutional disorder...without simultaneous disorder of general mental functions*". An individual could be low functioning in mathematics and yet have above average intelligence. According to Kosc, true dyscalculia can be measured by using the formula:

$$\text{Math Q (Quotient)} = \frac{\text{Mathematical age}}{\text{Chronological age}} \times 100$$

Individuals whose quotient was seventy to seventy-five or lower but who showed average or above average intelligence were said to display dyscalculia. Kosc also differentiated between dyscalculia and mathematical difficulties resulting from poor teaching, inadequate learning opportunity, and mental retardation. He classified true dyscalculia as consisting of symptoms that could be grouped into the following six categories (pp. 49–50):

1. Verbal dyscalculia – difficulty with verbal use of mathematical terms and symbols.
2. Practognistic dyscalculia – inability to recognize distinguishing features or to make comparisons of objects that vary on some dimension, for example, size.

3. Lexical dyscalculia – difficulty reading digits, symbols, or multidigit numbers.
4. Graphical dyscalculia – difficulty writing dictated numbers or copying symbols.
5. Ideognostical dyscalculia – difficulty comprehending mathematical ideas and making mental calculations.
6. Operational dyscalculia – difficulty completing basic operations of addition, subtraction, and so on, including confusion among the operations and the appropriate algorithm for each.

In addition, environmental factors may be responsible for a disability in mathematics.

Motivation

Children come to mathematics with a mind block that they will never be able to understand anything! The attitude of the learner is a major factor responsible for his inability to acquire concepts. Acquired skills may disappear due to lack of practice.

Poor Teaching

Poor quality teaching is another factor. Many teachers are not aware of how to teach mathematics or what sequential skills are required at the primary classes. Skills are taught in a fragmented manner. The emphasis is on rote learning which is disastrous for the learning disabled child. A much more meaningful approach will be to focus on applying reasoning skills to real-life problems, making inferences and setting hypotheses. Teachers tend to "overcorrect" the incorrect answer rather than praise the child for the correct steps.

Lack of Learning Readiness

Many children fail to acquire math concepts because they lack the cognitive maturity to understand them. For example, the ability to discriminate between numbers is related to the ability to discriminate between various sizes and shapes. If for some reason the child has not been able to master simple shape discrimination, he will encounter difficulties in the later stages as well when quantitative reasoning is required. In the early years these children seldom enjoy working with puzzles or blocks, have difficulty sorting and matching objects, and understanding the language ("more/less") of arithmetic. In the elementary classes, the child with problems in arithmetic will find it difficult to perform simple computational problems (Otto, McMenemy, & Smith, 1973).

Cawley *et al.* (1979) cited four specific reasons why children fail to learn mathematics and these deserve special attention: (1) incorrect instruction from teachers who have a limited knowledge of what alternative strategies to use; (2) the learner lacks the prerequisite skills needed to understand a concept; (3) the teacher pays attention to giving negative feedback related to incorrect answers and ignores any correct steps in the sequence; (4) failure to diagnose error patterns.

Wood (1980) suggested that many learning disabled children find the modern math approach particularly difficult to understand because of several reasons. First, they find the language and vocabulary used in modern math very difficult. Second, set notation presents them with directional problems. Third, many parents are unfamiliar with modern math and are unable to help their children at home.

Other researchers (Cawley *et al.*, 1979; Johnson and Myklebust, 1967; Lerner, 1981; and McLeod and Crump, 1978) examined a variety of related deficits that may compound the problem:

1. Deficits in auditory reception make it difficult to attach meaning to concepts presented orally.
2. Deficit in attention interferes with the ability to concentrate.
3. Problems in memory make recall difficult, for example, retrieving symbols and their meaning.
4. Verbal-related problems make it difficult to deal with tasks requiring verbal reasoning.
5. Perceptual errors (visuospatial and visuomotor) may cause incorrect visual representations.

6. Left-right confusion may occur: reading requires a left-to-right movement while many mathematical operations require the reverse.

Types of Mathematical Problems

Children with learning disabilities exhibit a variety of deficits in the area of mathematics.

Shape Discrimination

The ability to recognize and copy shapes is a basic skill, which develops fairly early. Lerner (1976) observes that shape discrimination may not come automatically to all children – some children may see a square as four separate lines. Children with a learning disability may find it difficult to use a form board in play activities and this confusion with shapes may effect their discrimination of numbers (for example, 2/4 and 6/9).

Size Discrimination

A large number of quantitative skills are based on the ability to discriminate between different sizes. Concrete concepts such *big, small, long, short* are very important for mastering the abstract concepts of *more, less, greater than, lesser than,* and other quantitative concepts. A problem is indicated in this area when they fail to identify the "biggest" tree, the "longest" pencil, the "shortest" boy, and so on. A child who cannot identify the larger box may later be unable to identify the larger of two numbers. More complex concepts like estimating the area or perimeter of an object also require size discrimination.

Sets and Numbers

A set is a family of objects, and anything within a set is called an element or member of that set. For example, tables, chairs, cupboards are all members of the set called furniture. Mathematically, sets have been used to help children count. Unfortunately most learning-disabled children do not understand the concept of a set and find it difficult to *categorize* objects according to a particular common quality. The number property of sets is often confused with the objects contained inside the set. For example, in Figure 7.1, many learning disabled children will see set A as squares, set B as circles, set C as triangles, and set D as stars, forgetting that set A goes with set D because both have four objects inside the set.

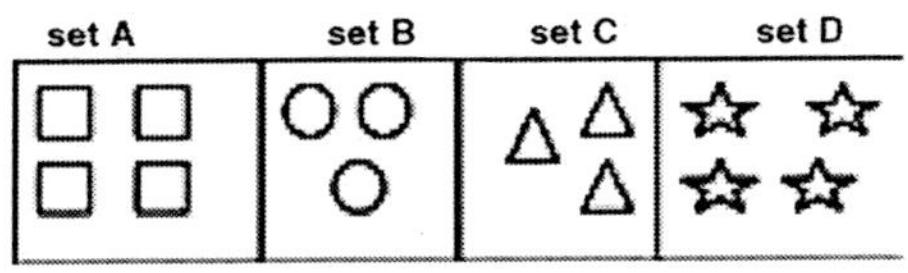

Figure 7.1: Set Matching

Counting each object, and associating the symbol 4 with the four stars will also be a problem for them. The language and specific terms used with set theory is also difficult for learning disabled children. *Equal sets, empty sets, and subsets* may be confusing and children may need experience with concrete objects before they are ready for this.

Counting

Counting is the most basic skill required for any kind of mathematical understanding. A child may have difficulty with counting because he has not understood the concept of one-to-one correspondence, for example, four pencils can be given out to four persons. According to Reisman (1978), a child should be asked to count a basket of apples. If the child counts in the two ways described in Figure 7.2, it indicates he still has to understand the concept of one-to-one correspondence.

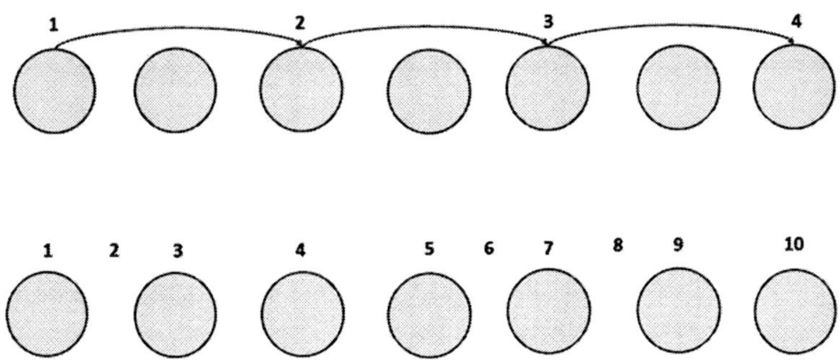

Figure 7.2: Counting Mistakes

Very often, children with learning disability simply cannot associate quantity with a numeral, for example, that the symbol 7 corresponds to 7 stars. The child may also have difficulties with ordinal numbers and not be able to indicate the third position in a row, the seventh day in the week or second month in the year.

Bereiter (1968, pp. 15–16) has listed some additional problems that children face when counting. Most of these tasks involve integrating a thought process with auditory or visual skills, which appears to be particularly difficult for learning disabled individuals.

- Counting perceptually dissimilar objects such as pans or stones differing greatly in size, vases of differing shapes, or drawn figures differing in both size and shape.
- Counting objects all visible at a glance but not touchable: trees or buildings at a distance, lights hanging from the ceiling, or panes on a window.
- Counting objects one must move about to count: beds, doors, bookcases in a house, or benches in a park.
- Counting the facets of a single object: sides of a cube, teeth in a gear, seams on a tire, corners on a stop sign, star, or a christmas tree ornament.
- Counting objects not simultaneously present: people who visited class, or animals seen on a nature walk.
- Counting classes of objects: kinds of flowers in garden, kinds of tropical fish in an aquarium, or brands of dog food in a grocery store.
- Counting subclasses of objects: red beads in bead assortment, blue-eyed children in class, or hoofed animals in a picture book.

Auditory-Visual Association

Just as reading is rendered more difficult because of an underlying language deficit, mathematical concepts appear problematic owing to the child's inability to associate the written with the visual symbols. Often children cannot associate the number name "sixteen" with the numeral 16. They may be unable to recall numbers during number dictation or identify numerals verbally. Memory deficits can aggravate the problem.

Place Value

The concept of place value – ones and tens – appears difficult to many children and more so to learning-disabled children who may be having problems with left-right orientation. These children may read the digit 63 as 6 and 3 or reverse it as 36. Or they may find it difficult to understand that the same digit (e.g., 7) may indicate different values according to how it is placed (e.g., 47, 17, or 744). Place value will naturally effect how the child solves addition and subtraction problems, especially those involving borrowing and carry-over.

Computing Skills

When the fundamental skills such as counting and one-to-one correspondence are not well established, the child is bound to have difficulty with simple computation. It is important to make learning disabled children understand the quantitative relationships between the different processes rather than depend on rote memorization. For example, multiplication is an extension of addition, subtraction is the inverse operation of addition, and division the inverse operation of multiplication. Children with learning disabilities must be given much more practice with concrete and manipulative materials. The use of number lines, and other ancillary aides must be encouraged.

Measurement, Money, Time

These three areas are important for functional living and many learning disabled children find it difficult to handle concepts of measurement and money in adult life. High-school mathematics which uses perimeters, volume, bar graphs, pie-charts and so on adds to the confusion. Similarly when learning about money, students may get anxious when asked to deal with coins and change rupees into smaller denominations. Peterson (1973) suggests that poor sequence of time and the complexity of the clock's number system contribute to poor time-telling skills. Learning disabled children may find it difficult to tell time because they cannot discriminate between numbers like 6 and 9 or because of simple counting difficulty. The terminology used – "six-thirty," "three-fifteen," "quarter past one" – is equally confusing.

They may also find it difficult to understand why 6 o' clock occurs twice a day.

Language

It is surprising how most teachers take it for granted that the mathematical language and terms used are easily understood by children. Table 7.1 lists some quantitative terms which children often find confusing.

Table 7.1: Common Quantitative Terms

add	graph
algorithm	greater than
angle	increase
area	less than
associate property	measure
average	minus
cardinal number	multiply
circle	number
circumference	numerator
commutative property	one - to - one correspondence
counting	ordinal number
decimal	parallel
degree	per cent
denominator	place value
diameter	plus
digit	product
distributive property	rectangle
divide	remainder
dividend	same as
divisor	set
equal	solution
equation	subtract
error	symbol
estimate	triangle
fraction	zero

Source: Learning Disabilities: Concepts and Characteristics. By K. Wailers and J.R. McLoughlin, Columbus, Ohio: Charles E. Morrill. 1979.

A good idea would be to work specifically on mathematical terms asking the child to apply them to a variety of real-life situations. Learning disabled children who have receptive language problems will also find it difficult to understand quantitative concepts such as *before, after, fewer than. lesser than, more* or *greater than*. Some children may not be able to differentiate mathematical symbols and signs such as +, ×, –. The equal sign is often perceived as two subtraction signs. It is important that the student recognize and understand the meaning of the signs in order to solve any problems.

Problem Solving

Children with a learning disability find it very difficult to solve word problems both owing to a reading deficit and a lack of analysis and reasoning skills. Most word problems involve a fair degree of abstract thinking and inferential reasoning and in the absence of concrete manipulative objects the child is unable to tackle these problems. Another area of difficulty arises from not knowing which operation or process to use – does the problem require addition or division? The child must be given repeated practice to avoid using a trial-and-error method and learn to develop a systematic approach to problem solving.

Assessment of Mathematical Disorders

Formal Assessments

Formal tests are available commercially to test both general skills and specific areas of deficit. Most standardized achievement tests have subsections that deal with arithmetic, geometry, problem solving, and so on. Standardized achievement tests provide an overall measure of arithmetic achievement and are not intended to assess specific skills. In case a more detailed assessment is required, the teacher should use diagnostic tests, which assess basic arithmetic operations, decimals, fractions, and so on. Table 7.2 and Table 7.3 list some of the more commonly used tests.

Table 7.2: Achievement Tests with Arithmetic Sections

Name of Test	Age level	Arithmetic skill evaluated
Peabody Individual Achievement Test-Revised (PIAT-R)	5 to 22–11 years	100 multiple-choice items to test knowledge and application of math concepts and facts.
Woodcock Johnson Tests of Achievement-Revised, 4th ed. (WJ-IV)	4 years to adult	Computation; Math fluency
Wide Range Achievement Test-4 (WRAT-4)	5 years to adult	Computation

Table 7.3: Diagnostic Arithmetic Tests

Name of Test	Age level	Arithmetic skill evaluated
Test of Early Mathematics Ability, TEMA-3	3 to 8–11 years	72 items covering school-taught concepts and skills.
KeyMath-Revised interpreting Normative-Update (KeyMath-R/NU)	5 to 22 years	13 subtests in estimation, data, problem solving etc.
Test of Mathematical Abilities, TOMA-2	8 to 18–11 years	Story problems, Computation, Attitude to Math.

Informal Assessments

Teacher-made informal tests are very useful because they are target-specific, practical and easy to implement. However, they must be well constructed and the teacher must know the relation between the skill to be assessed and the nature of the problem. Assessment must vary across written assignments, oral work and board work. Encourage the child to verbalize and explain the steps he is following when solving a problem. He should not be helped or guided at this stage. The end-result of the data collected should be a comprehensive assessment of the child's current and future needs, his developmental readiness for the task, mathematical skills available, and expectations from the system.

Guidelines for Informal assessment*

1. Obtain the student's instructional history in mathematics, and in other subjects. It is important to know if the child has always been performing poorly in mathematics, what methods have been used earlier, whether they worked, and any other related factors. Work samples can be collected and errors analyzed. An error analysis chart is provided in Appendix 3.
2. Assess the student's attitude towards school in general, and towards mathematics in particular. Does he feel it will help him later in life, or does he associate it with repeated failure?
3. Assess the student's other interests. Identifying his likes and dislikes, hobbies and interests will allow the teacher to select effective reinforcers.
4. Evaluate the student's behaviours specially attention span, learning styles, time taken to complete a task, and so on. The teacher can observe if the child looks puzzled, or counts on his fingers under the table.
5. Check on why the child was referred and by whom. Sometimes when parents refer the child, they tend have unrealistic expectations about their child's ability, and overreact to low marks.
6. Rule out the presence of any sensory deficits. Both vision and hearing must be checked.
7. Assess the child's general cognitive abilities. The teacher needs to estimate the discrepancy between expected and actual performance. Informal Piagetian tasks may also be used to decide the student's stage of cognitive development, for example whether the child can sequence events or sets of objects; classify objects according to common attributes (sets and subsets) and so on.

*Teachers interested in additional guidelines for constructing informal arithmetic tests should refer to Wallace and Kauffman (1978), Wallace and Larsen (1978), and Moran (1978).

Instructional Methods for Teaching Mathematics

Most teachers are somewhat intimidated when it comes to remedying mathematical deficits in learning disabled children. In a typical classroom situation, teachers complain the syllabus does not permit them to devote as much time to practicing concepts, as they would like. Concepts are introduced at a fairly rapid rate before the child has really mastered them and the traditional "drill and practice" methods are left for parents to carry out at home. Parents in turn complain that they know little of "modern Math" and cannot help their children in any way. Finally, it is the child who suffers and very soon develops the all-too familiar "math phobia." There are many different commercial math programs available but teachers must know which program is best suited for effective learning. With learning disabled students, it is preferable not to use a "discovery" approach where the teacher creates an open-ended environment and acts only as a guide leaving the child to discover the solution. It is far better to use a structured format and present each task in a sequence of steps, leaving as little as possible to random guessing on the part of the learner. With most learning disabled children, it helps if the teacher first explicitly states the rule or principle and gives examples of that rule (the deductive approach) rather than allow the child to work on examples and state the rule (inductive thinking). Above all, there are certain general principles of good teaching that apply to all remedial work and to all students. Teachers should not lose sight of these principles. Often, strategies based on commonsense and practice are the most effective.

Houck (1984, p. 369) suggests that the following tasks are critical for instruction in mathematics:

1. *Sets* – grouping of objects or ideas that have some common attribute. For example, all squares in one set, and circles in another.
2. *Matching set members or elements* – determining whether each member of one set has a "partner" or if they do not match up. We call the former case an instance of one-to-one correspondence.
3. *Number* – the words used to describe the concept of "how many." The actual word may change with different languages, yet the concept of "two ness" remains the same.
4. *Number names or numerals* – recognition and later reproduction of symbols that represent a specific number.

5. *Ordering* – recognizing the relationship of one or more than or less than in the numerical sequence and the idea of a few more, a few less, many more, many less as comparative statements for sets containing a differing number of elements.
6. *Counting* – mental recognition that when we count, we are matching the total elements with the number label we have given to the set. Thus when we count three, we could go back and match the objects we counted with the mental elements that we have come to know as "three ness."
7. *Place value in base ten* – a numerical value is associated with each position in a written numeral. Each digit represents a product of the place value and the specific numeral that occupies the position.

Some General Remedial Principles

Understand the student Each student comes to the learning task with an attitude born out of past failure with math. The teacher must first determine what the starting point is going to be, whether prerequisite skills and concepts have been acquired, and whether these can be applied spontaneously to real-life problems. Have the student verbalize his thought processes in working specific problems.

Begin with concrete experiences The concepts of telling time, fractions, geometry, division, and measurement are more easily understood when concrete manipulative objects are used. Children master abstract concepts far better when they actually "do" problems with their hands.

Relate math to real-life problems Children learn much faster when they can see the relationship between worksheets and problems in real-life. For example, learning division increases the learner's interest and motivation when applied to dividing housework between members of a family; or, dividing time into study and playtime activities. When one teaches for meaning, the student internalizes the concepts and is able to transfer them to real-life problem solving.

Use materials effectively Two fairly new recent individualized intervention programs for young children are the Mathematics Recovery program

(Wright, Martland, & Stafford, 2000) and the Numeracy Recovery program (Dowker, 2001, 2003). They have some interesting features. The Mathematics Recovery program is much more intensive than the Numeracy Recovery program, and places more emphasis on methods of counting and number representation. It was designed in Australia by Wright (Wright *et al.*, 2000). Teachers provide intensive (30 minutes per day) individualized intervention to low-attaining 6 and 7 year olds over 12–14 weeks. Teachers reported that children improved very significantly, they could apply ideas to classroom teaching, and it helped them gain a better understanding of children's math development.

The Numeracy Recovery program (Dowker 2001, 2003) was piloted with 6 and 7 year olds in Oxford. Children identified as having problems in arithmetic received 30 minutes a week of training on the particular components with which they were having difficulty. The Numeracy program emphasizes estimation and derived fact strategy use.

Instructional Strategies

There is very little research to describe early interventions to *prevent* mathematical disability in struggling students. More research has been done for older students (Baker, Gersten, & Lee, 2002; Gersten *et al.*, in press). The goals of early intensive intervention however are quite clear:

- To increase fluency and accuracy with basic arithmetic facts.
- To develop more mature and efficient counting strategies
- To develop number sense.

It is better to use a variety of approaches rather than look for one single method that works best. Young children benefit from direct instruction in the use of strategies. It is also important to increase opportunities for generalization as it takes time for younger children to learn how to generalize. Recently Jordan *et al.* (2003) and Robinson *et al.* (2002) have argued that children must learn to use calculation principles or "short cuts." For example, 2 + 2 = 4 so 2 + 3 = 5. Or, 6 + 4 = 10 so 10–6 = 4. This kind of instruction is much more productive than rote drill which places a heavy demand on memory, an area of weakness for many learning-disabled students. Mental calculation short cuts help children develop fluency as well as number sense. According to Robinson *et al.* (2002), number sense is a kind of knowledge about numbers and it should be teachable, like phonemic awareness. Based on implementation research (Gersten, Chard, Griffiths, Katz, & Bryant, 2003), we would only recommend the whole-class activities such as practise in "counting on," listen to coins being dropped in a box and counting, practice counting backwards, practice in linking addition and subtraction to the manipulation of objects. These activities are easy to do with a small group of children and help build a sense of number.

Students need to learn the very abstract language of mathematics before they can express their ideas; thus learning the vocabulary of mathematics seems another critical piece of early intervention.

When choosing the most appropriate program teachers should question whether the program is well sequenced and addresses stage-appropriate skills. The overall appearance of the materials should be uncluttered; directions should be simple and clearly understood; and, it should link real-life situations to the concepts taught. The most expensive program need not necessarily be the best. Numerous mathematics textbooks, materials, and manipulatives are available to assist teachers in providing instruction to students with learning disability. However, textbooks, materials, and manipulatives should be carefully evaluated before they are used in the classroom to ensure that they meet student needs. Teachers can adapt and enhance the content of traditional textbooks to best meet the students' needs. *Appendix 3 lists resources for parents and teachers.*

Modifications for Students with Learning Disabilities

Textbooks may need to be modified to meet individual needs of students with a learning disability. In this respect, it is important to keep in mind the student's instructional level and IEP goals and objectives. Students with learning disability must be taught specific strategies for math problem-solving. They may need (a) extra practice to reach mastery; (b) shortened assignments, as opposed to the 30 to 50 problems given in the textbook and on worksheets; and (c) maintenance practice on previously mastered skills to ensure continued mastery of the concept. The following five steps can be used to modify a math unit (Silbert *et al.*, 1981).

1. Prioritize the objectives of the unit and set mastery levels.
2. Select problem-solving strategies.
3. Construct teaching formats for major skills and for preskills when necessary.
4. Select practice examples.
5. Design worksheets or select pages of the text to provide review of previously taught skills.

References

Baker, S., Gersten, R. & Lee, D. (2002). A synthesis of empirical research on teaching mathematics to low achieving students. *The Elementary School Journal,* 103, 51–73.

Bereiter, C. & Scardamalia, M.(1981). From conversation to composition: The role of instruction in a developmental process. In R. Glaser (Ed.), *Advances in instructional psychology* (Vol. 2, pp. 132–165). Hillsdale, NJ: Erlbaum.

Bereiter, C. (1968). *Arithmetic and mathematics.* San Rafael, Calif.: Dimensions.

Bryant, D.P., Bryant, B.R. & Hammill, D.D. (2000). Characteristic behaviors of students with learning disabilities who have teacher-defined math weaknesses. *Journal of Learning Disabilities,* 33, 168–179.

Cawley, J.F., Goodstein, H.A. Fitzmaurice, A.M., Lepore, A., Sedlak, R. & Althaus, V. (1976). *Project Math.* Tulsa: Educational Programs Corp.

Cohn, Robert (1961). Dyscalculia. *Archives of Neurology,* 4, 301–307.

Danforth, M. (1978). Aids for learning mathematics. *Arithmetic Teacher,* 26, 4.

Dehaene, S. (1997). *The number sense: How the mind creates mathematics.* New York: Oxford University Press.

Desoete, A., Roeyers, H. & De Clercq, A. (2004). Children with mathematical learning disabilities in Belgium. *Journal of Learning Disabilities,* 37, 32–41.

Dowker, A.D. (1998). Individual differences in arithmetical development. In C. Donlan (Ed.), *The development of mathematical skills* (pp. 275–302). London: Taylor and Francis.

Dowker, A.D. (2001). Numeracy recovery: A pilot scheme for early intervention with young children with numeracy difficulties. *Support for Learning,* 16, 6–10.

Dowker, A.D. (2003). Interventions in numeracy: Individualized approaches. In I. Thompson (Ed.), *Enhancing primary mathematics teaching* (pp. 127–138). Maidenhead, UK: Open University Press.

Fuchs, L.S., Fuchs, D. & Prentice, K. (2004). Responsiveness to mathematical problem-solving instruction: Comparing students at risk of mathematics disability with and without risk of reading disability. *Journal of Learning Disabilities,* 37, 293–306.

Geary, D. (1990). A componential analysis of an early learning deficit in mathematics. *Journal of Experimental Child Psychology,* 33, 386–404.

Geary, D.C. (1993). Mathematical disabilities: Cognitive, neuropsychological, and genetic components. *Psychological Bulletin,* 114, 345–362.

Geary, D.C. (2004). Mathematics and learning disabilities. *Journal of Learning Disabilities,* 37, 4–15.

Gersten, R., Chard, D., Baker, S.Jayanthi, M., Flojo, J. & Lee, D. (under review). *Experimental and quasi-experimental research on instructional approaches for teaching mathematics to students with learning disabilities:* A research synthesis. Review of Educational Research.

Gersten, R., Chard, D., Griffiths, R., Katz, R. & Bryant, D. (2003, April). *Methods and materials for reaching students in early and intermediate mathematics.* Paper presented at the Council for Exceptional Children, Seattle, WA.

Ginsburg, H.P. & Baroody, A.J. (1994). *Test of early mathematical ability* (2nd edition). Austin, Tx: PRO-ED.

Hacaen, H. (1967). Brain mechanisms suggested by studies of parietal lobes. In C.H. Millikan (chairman) and F.L. Darley (ed.) *Brain Mechanisms Underlying Speech and Language.* New York: Grune & Stratton, Inc., pp. 146–166.

Hanich, L., Jordan, N., Kaplan, D. & Dick, J. (2001). Performance across different areas of mathematical cognition in children with learning disabilities. *Journal of Educational Psychology,* 93, 615–626.

Houck, Cherry K. (1984). *Learning Disabilities: Understanding Concepts, Characteristics and Issues.* Prentice-Hall, Inc. Englewood Cliffs, New Jersey.

Johnson, D.J. & Myklebust, H.R. (1967). *Learning disabilities: Educational principles and practices.* New York: Grune & Stratton.

Jordan, N., Hanich, L. & Kaplan, D. (2003). A longitudinal study of mathematical competencies in children with specific mathematics difficulties versus children with comorbid mathematics and reading disabilities. *Child Development,* 74, 834–850.

Jordan, N.C. & Hanich, L.B. (2000). Mathematical thinking in second grade children with different forms of LD. *Journal of Learning Disabilities,* 33, 567–578.

Koppitz, E.M. (1971). *Children with learning disabilities: A five-year follow-up study.* New York: Grune & Stratton.

Kosc, L. (1974). Developmental dyscalculia. *Journal of learning disabilities,* 7, 3, 46–59.

Lerner, J.W. (1981). *Learning Disabilities: Theories, Diagnosis, and Teaching Strategies* (3rd ed.). Boston: Houghton-Mifflin Company.

Luria, A. (1980). *Higher Cortical Functions in Man* (2nd ed.). New York: Basic Books, Inc., Publishers.

McLeod, T. & Crump, D. (1978). The relationship of visuospatial skills and verbal ability to learning disabilities in mathematics. *Journal of learning Disabilities,* 11, 4, 53–57.

Miles, T.R., Haslum, M.N. & Wheeler, T.J. (2001). The mathematical abilities of dyslexic ten-year-olds. *Annals of Dyslexia,* 51, 299–321.

Moran, M.R. (1978). *Assessment of the exceptional learner in the regular classroom.* Denver: Love Publishing.

Otto, W., McMenemy, R.A. & Smith, R.J. (1973). *Corrective and remedial teaching.* Boston: Houghton Mifflin.

Peterson, D. (1973). *Functional mathematics for the mentally retarded. Columbus,* Ohio: Charles E. Merrill.

Piaget, J. & Inhelder B. (1969). *The Psychology of the Child.* New York: Basic Books, Inc., Publishers.

Reisman, F.K. (1978). *A Guide to the Diagnostic Teaching of Arithmetic (2nd ed.).* Columbus, Ohio: Charles E. Merrill.

____________(1977). *Diagnostic Teaching of Elementary School Mathematics.* Chicago: Rand McNally College Publishing Co.

Resnick, L.B. & Ford, W.W. (1989). *The psychology of mathematics for instruction*. Hillsdale, N.J.: Lawrence Erlbaum Associates.

Robinson, C., Menchetti, B. & Torgeson, J. (2002). Toward a two-factor theory of one type of mathematics disabilities. *Learning Disabilities Research & Practice*, 17, 81–89.

Siegler, R.S. & Shrager, J. (1984). Strategy choice in addition and subtraction: How do children know what to do? In C. Sophian (Ed.), *Origins of cognitive skills* (pp. 229–293). Mahwah, NJ: Erlbaum.

Silbert, J., Carnine, D. & Stein, M. (1981). *Organizing mathematics instruction*. Columbus, OH: Merrill.

Wallace, G. & Kaufmann, J.M. (1978). *Teaching children with learning problems* (2nd ed.). Columbus, Ohio: Charles E. Merrill.

Wallace, G. & Larsen, S.C. (1978). *Educational Assessment of Learning Problems: Testing for Teachers.* Boston: Allyn & Bacon.

Wallace, G. & McLoughlin, J.A. (1979). *Learning Disabilities: Concepts and Characteristics* (2nd ed.). Columbus, Ohio: Charles E. Merrill.

Wood, M.H. (1980). Modern Math & the LD child. *Academic Therapy*, 15, 3, 279–290.

Wright, R., Martland, J. & Stafford, A. (2000). *Early numeracy: Assessment for teaching and intervention*. London, Chapman.

CHAPTER 8

Learning Disabilities in Adolescents and Adults

Introduction

College programs for learning disabled persons emerged in response to the educational needs of learning disabled youngsters and adults. An increasing number of older dyslexics wish to establish themselves in professional careers, obtain more knowledge, and continue learning. Fortunately, the path to a college education runs much more smoothly than could be anticipated. Legislation and social awareness both helped to establish some rights for this population in other countries. AB-77 (Assembly Bill No. 77) is a California state law that was passed in 1976 to ensure that handicapped students received appropriate services in college. It goes one step beyond PL 94–142, which applies only to handicapped students until secondary school. The special services mentioned should be of interest to us in this country: counseling, assistance when registering, college orientation, assessment for academic and vocational placement, special educational materials, tutoring; arrangement for class lectures to be photocopied or tape-recorded; modification of the class timetables; extended time to complete course requirements; and other support services. Especially important is the stipulation that no program shall be denied to a handicapped student solely on the basis of his handicap. In India, however, higher education for learning disabled adolescents and adults remains an extremely neglected area. Currently, there are no services known to exist at the University level to meet their needs.

Identifying the Learning Disabled Adult

Assessing the adult dyslexic is a far more complex issue than identifying younger children. Adults bring with them different experiences –

some may never read for pleasure; others may have learned to cope very well using technology as an aid. So a lot depends on the previous knowledge and interventions received, if any. Instead of using one single test, a battery of tests may be required to detect specific gaps in their development. The one persistent quality that continues to manifest itself even in older dyslexic adults is the phonologic deficit, which affects the speed of reading. Drawing from her own research, Sally Shaywitz (Overcoming Dyslexia, pg.162, 2003) points out that "Brain imaging studies indicate adult dyslexics never switch over to the automatic reading circuit necessary for fluent reading." Older dyslexic students do learn to read, and often with good comprehension, but they lack fluency. Researchers have established that college students are accurate but slower readers, implying that accuracy comes at a price! Older dyslexic readers tend to use contextual clues rather than phonetic rules when reading. Assessment tests for young adults must test both for fluency and for accuracy. If an adult has never been assessed previously, it is critical to obtain the complete educational history. Usually, such a history will indicate that the person had difficulty reading throughout school, had difficulty with language, had a poor handwriting, and perhaps relied on a different set of coping skills than his peers. There is bound to be a great deal of disparity in the educational background of learning disabled adults. Some may have got there with no help at

A Learning Disability Often Persists into Adulthood

all; others may have received specialized assistance and support. Still others may possibly have dropped out of school and headed towards a National Open School system to complete their education.

How a person reads aloud is the most important clue to dyslexia in older persons. Timed reading tests such as the Nelson-Denny Reading Tests and tests from the GORT-4 can further help establish an accurate diagnosis.

College Education for the Learning Disabled

An important question that troubles most parents is whether their child will be able to function as an independent adult. Although dyslexia has no cure, many youngsters grow up to complete their education from reputed universities, professional schools, and hold their own in the workforce. Interventions are usually more successful with young adults because they want to do better and are motivated to reach their goals.

Getting Ready for College

- Have open discussions with your child about what learning disability means and how this could impact career choices.
- Make information available so that the youngster can better understand his own strengths and weaknesses.
- Highlight the achievement of other dyslexic adults and point out how they went on to achieve and contribute to society.
- Praise your child's perseverance and struggle and seek out methods that would work for him.
- Prepare the faculty for how they can better support your child in college.

It is often helpful for learning disabled adults to take additional courses to prepare for the demands of college life. For example, a "study skills" course teaches how to read college-level textbooks, develop strategies for remembering important information, prepare papers, use the library, and take examinations. Another helpful course would be one that addresses the fundamentals of communication. It would help the students to cope with college life at many levels – emotional, social and academic. A basic reading and writing course that focuses on oral expression, listening skills, grammar, paragraph development, word attack skills, vocabulary development would be useful.

The faculty must know what they can expect from learning disabled students. Provide teachers with a one-page outline, explaining the nature of learning disabilities and what they can do to make college life more amenable for the learning disabled student. For example, they can provide an outline of the lecture, simplify the level of the language, and teach definitions and terms more carefully.

The attitude of the faculty is undoubtedly the single most important factor in ensuring success in college. In most foreign countries, each college or University has a well-staffed Office for Students with Learning Disabilities, which handles all requests for special services. The office acts as a liaison between the staff and the student. Unfortunately in India we are still very far from providing this kind of support. The learning disabled adult is dependent on the family for moral and financial support and few options or alternatives are available.

Auxiliary Aids and Services to assist learning disabled adults in college

- Use books on tape, calculators, and computers. Remember, it is time consuming to listen back to recorded lectures.
- Recorded textbooks can be ordered from the National Library Service for the Blind and Physically Handicapped (NLS), the Library of Congress, 1291 Taylor Street NW, Washington D.C. 20542, USA. The books are supplied free of cost. However, practice will be needed to extract information efficiently from these "talking books."
- Note takers can sit in during the lectures and "take notes."
- Alternative testing arrangements may be needed during examinations.
- Students can take the same examination but with extended time limits.

- For students who have difficulty reading, questions can be pre-recorded; or, a writer can be used to read out the questions and scribe the answers as is done for visually impaired students.
- Permission may be obtained to make a PowerPoint presentation in class.

Accommodations or Modifications

Students with learning disability may require some kind of modification or accommodations in their curriculum. Accommodations help them keep pace with their peers and allow their true potential to shine through. Several accommodations are available throughout school but are more easily available at college level. This could be because school life tends to be more rigid and rule bound, whereas college instruction lends itself more easily to innovative approaches to teaching and learning. Evaluation procedures in college tend to be flexible and more open than in schools. Many people argue that providing accommodations encourages learned disabled individuals not to work harder, and gives them an unfair advantage over their peers. Nothing could be further from the truth. Some accomodations (such as extra time) are critical to college success and, in fact, level the playing field for the learning disabled student.

Extra Time for Tests and Examinations

For learning disabled students, extra time is very important because most of them are slow readers and need more time to process information. The extra time allows them to read the question paper thoroughly and edit their answers before submission. This is especially important when taking 'timed tests' such as the SATs prior to college admission. The amount of extra time required varies from school to school but most Boards in India do allow up to 15 minutes extra time per hour. Learning disabled students should be taught how to use this extra time wisely, and without feeling embarrassed.

Colleges Should Offer Support to the Adult Dyslexic

Books on Audio

Older learning-disabled persons must be able to access factual knowledge at the same rate as their peers. Since they continue to be slow readers even as adults, books recorded on audio will help them keep pace. Listening to audio recordings helps the reader focus on the meaning of the text and helps him to acquire vocabulary required for a professional course. Several organizations across the world offer books on audio. Parents can contact RFB & D of Princeton, New Jersey (www.rfbd.org) for a list of textbooks available with them. Books on audio are also available at www.audible.com.

Exemption from a Second Language

Schools expect their students to learn one or more foreign languages and this can be difficult for many learning disabled individuals. The CBSE and ICSE Boards of Education in India permit exemption from a second language (even if it is that child's native language).

Use of the Computer

Though some learning disabled students do not enjoy keyboarding, the computer comes as a real blessing for most. It allows them to use a variety of software programs that enhance their ability to read, write and spell, thereby allowing them to compete in school. Computer programs are also available to help with courses that require figures, graphs and illustrations. Laptop computers can be used in the classroom for making notes. Lectures can also be recorded or photocopied.

Appendix 5 presents a synopsis of accommodations available to students with a learning disability.

Instructional Methods

Adults do particularly well with group instruction and benefit from learning from one another. Sessions can extend for about 2 hours, three to four times a week. Regular attendance is a critical factor in progress – the professional lives of many adults may lead them to be irregular and the dropout rate is usually quite high.

Some excellent programs for adult dyslexics are:

- Language!
- The Wilson Reading System
- Starting Over

These are described in greater detail in Appendix 5.

Reference

Shaywitz, S. (2003). Overcoming Dyslexia. Albert A. Knopf.

Section-III

Assessment and Remediation

Chapter 9

The Assessment Process

What is Assessment?

Assessment is the systematic process of collecting information about a child, his past and current levels of performance, his strengths and weaknesses, in order to help make better educational decisions. Assessment needs to be relevant to the teaching goals and interventions that the child will receive.

Ideally, the purpose of testing is to identify why a child is not learning and define what steps can be taken to solve his problem. Assessment is directly linked with how one will go about helping the child. It is linked with the intervention methods one will use. It simplifies teaching by clearly outlining long term and short-term objectives, and specifying what materials are to be used. As far as possible, testing of a learning disabled child must be done on an individual basis and not in a group because the characteristics of each child are unique. The information collected must be relevant and of practical help in the classroom. Moreover, the assessment is not an "once-in-a-lifetime" stamp but must be repeated at suitable intervals so that decisions can be changed and new goals set. Assessment helps parents to better understand their child's problems and adjust their expectations on the basis of the assessment data.

In the West, an important goal of assessment has been administrative, to provide "the most appropriate placement" for the child. Schools receive funds for children with special needs, and they are in fact mandated by the law to provide testing services for the child, if so required. Over the last few decades testing has become an integral part of most American schools. An unfortunate fall-out has been an unproductive overemphasis on intelligence tests as the sole indicator of a child's ability. In fact, assessment has come full circle in the United States with more and more states insisting that indiscriminate use of tests should be banned because they are "culturally biased," unfair, and stigmatize a child for life.

In India, the history of assessment is still in its infancy. If anything, we are at the other end of the spectrum, with schools reluctant to acknowledge the constructive role of assessment Teachers and parents alike view assessment with suspicion, especially since many schools use it as a convenient tool to have a "difficult" child removed from school. It is less common to find schools using a multi-disciplinary team of professionals to define a child's educational needs. One can only hope that as an awareness of learning disability increases, the field of educational testing too will grow in India.

Factors Affecting Assessment

A major factor that makes it difficult to assess a learning disabled child is the confusing nature of the disability itself. The category of "learning disability" continues to be ill-defined (see Chapter 1) and tends to act as a dumping ground for all kinds of learning problems. The absence of any clear-cut criteria adds to the confusion. In addition, there is a great deal of variation in characteristics among learning-disabled individuals, which makes assessment difficult.

The absence of testing instruments relevant to Indian students is another major drawback. Most tests are designed for native English speakers and have items which lie outside the cultural experience of the average Indian student. For example, pictures of igloos, snow boots, hot dogs, and so on.

Teacher training does not adequately prepare teachers to understand and interpret the test results. Assessments can be expensive, too.

On the other hand, a good, comprehensive assessment saves a lot of time and allows timely remedies to be put in place. For many families, the diagnosis of 'learning disability' actually comes as a relief. As one mother described it, "Finally, I knew what was wrong with my child.

She was not lazy or stupid but had difficulty processing words. Once I knew why she was struggling so hard to read, I could start helping her."

Approaches to Assessment

Two approaches are generally used to describe testing – formal and informal. Formal testing uses standardized tests while informal testing uses non-standardized tests.

Formal Assessment

Formal assessment uses standardized tests, which demand a high degree of uniformity in administration and interpretation. They allow comparison of students of the same age or grade, and can be used individually or in groups. It is generally expected that standardized tests select items of high technical quality, provide explicit directions for administration and scoring, and outline technical information related to the instrument's adequacy. One of the most important advantages of a standardized test is that it allows one to compare an individual's (or group's) ability with a normative sample (a sample drawn from the population). When selecting a standardized test, certain cautions must be kept in mind. The test manual must be carefully reviewed to ensure the test is used for the purpose it was intended. Teachers must know why they are testing, which test to select, and how the results will be used. A test need not be the best one simply because it is popular or expensive. Teachers should be sensitive to technical factors like the *reliability* and *validity* of tests. A test is said to be reliable if the scores obtained are consistent over repeated administrations. It is valid if it truly measures what it proposes to measure. Training in the use of standardized tests is always required. Interpretation of scores too, is a fairly skilled process as most tests yield many different kinds of scores, which can be confusing. For example, standardized tests, raw scores, grade equivalent scores, age equivalents, percentiles, and standard scores. Scores should never be over generalized, that is, applied to something for which the test was never intended. To understand what each of these scores means, and for more information on how to choose appropriate tests, the reader can refer to *Standards for Educational and Psychological Testing, 1999.*

Formal tests generally measure three main areas of development: (1) General intelligence and aptitude; (2) Achievement; and (3) Behaviour and Personality. Some of the best known tests are listed in Table 9.1.

Table 9.1: Formal Assessments Used for Testing Purposes

Content Area	Name of Test	Purpose	Age Range	Time to Administer
Cognitive ability and Intelligence	Stanford-Binet Intelligence Scales	Individually administered assessment of intelligence and cognitive abilities. Needs training to administer and score.	2 years-adult	5 minutes per test
	Wechsler Adult Intelligence Scale-4th ed. (WAIS-IV)	Individually administered assessment of intelligence and cognitive abilities. Needs training to administer and score.	16 years-adult	60–75 minutes
	Wechsler Intelligence Scale for Children-5th ed. (WISC-V)	Individually administered assessment of intelligence and cognitive abilities. Needs training to administer and score.	6 years-16.11	30–60 minutes
	Slosson Intelligence Test	Designed for use as a quick estimate of general verbal cognitive ability. All the items are presented in question and answer format.	4 years and over	10–20 minutes
Language	PPVT-4: Peabody Picture Vocabulary Test, Fourth Edition	Measures receptive language	2.6 years-adult	10 to 15 minutes

Content Area	Name of Test	Purpose	Age range	Time to Administer
	Conner's Rating Scale Behaviour Assessment System for Children-3rd ed. (BASC-3)	Measures attention deficits. Uses rating scales to measure behaviours and emotions. Parents, teachers and students can evaluate behaviours.	4 years-adult	5–10 minutes 10–20 minutes
Achievement Skills	Wide Range Achievement Tests-4th ed. (WRAT-4)	Measures academic skills in reading, spelling, math, computation.	5 years-adult	15–45 minutes
	Woodcock Johnson Tests of Achievement 4th ed. (WJ-IV)	Measures scholastic aptitude, oral language and achievement	4 years to adult	55–65 minutes
Visual-Motor	Beery developmental Test of Visual Motor Integration	Designed to assess visual perception, visual memory, and visuoconstructive abilities	2–15 years	
	Benton Visual-retention Test, 5th edition		8 years to adult	Not reported
Ability and discrete skills	DTLA-5: Detroit Tests of Learning Aptitude, 5th Edition	Measures basic abilities, and also shows the effects of language, attention, and motor abilities on test performance.	6 years to 17 years	40 minutes to 2 hours
Language	Illinois Test of Psycholinguistic Abilities, Revised Edition	Designed to measure acquisition and use of language.	4 years to 8 years	60 minutes

General Intelligence Tests

Intelligence tests measure general ability and level of functioning in areas considered to be indicative of intelligent behaviour. Usually, these areas include comprehension, memory, vocabulary, reasoning, and general knowledge. The best-known intelligence tests are probably the Wechsler Intelligence Scales and the Stanford-Binet Intelligence Scale. The three Wechsler Scales are designed for different ages and must be administered by a trained psychologist.

The Woodcock-Johnson Psycho-Educational Battery (Woodcock and Johnson, 1977), Illinois Test of Psycholinguistic Abilities (Kirk *et al.*, 1974) and Detroit Tests of Learning Aptitude (Baker and Leland, 1967) are other well-known ability tests. The TONI (Test of Non-Verbal Intelligence) is used frequently with children who are not native English speakers or may have suspected language delays.

Achievement Tests

Achievement tests assess how a child performs in specific academic areas such as arithmetic, writing, and reading. They provide information about a student's academic skills in comparison to other students of the same age and grade. They are often referred to as 'diagnostic tests' because they help to identify specific areas of weakness and strength. The three most widely used achievement tests are the Wide Range Achievement Test (WRAT-4, (Jastak and Jastak, 1965); Peabody Individual Achievement Test (PIAT, Dunn and Markwardt, 1970) and the Woodcock-Johnson Tests of Achievement (WJ-IV). The tasks in each of these differ and the teacher must be alert to these differences because a child's performance can vary from test to test owing to differences in the testing format. For example, both the WRAT and the WJ-IV require the student to write the spelling of words while the PIAT requires selection of the correct spelling from four given choices.

Criterion-referenced tests are another type of achievement test which measure the extent to which a child has acquired a particular skill or material. Instead of comparing the child to others, these tests look at how the child currently performs in respect to the skill being assessed. The Keymath Diagnostic Arithmetic test (Connolly *et al.*, 1976) and the Brigance Diagnostic inventory of Essential Skills (Brigance, 1979) are good examples.

Behavioural and Personality Tests

These tests measure emotional and social development, motivation and affective attitudes. Unfortunately, test items tend to be "normed" on typical, middle-class white populations and may not be relevant to social norms and behavioural expectations in India.

Informal Assessment

Informal tests are non-standardized procedures used by teachers and other professionals to collect information. The advantage of informal tests is that they are simple to construct, administer and score. They are targeted at a specific objective and are of greater value for making instructional decisions. However in order to be effective, these tests too must be systematic, structured and designed along scientific principles. The most frequently used informal procedures are observations, interviews, questionnaires, and tests.

Observations

In a typical Indian classroom setting, the teacher works with about 45 to 50 students. Despite the large classroom size she is the best observer of the child's performance. She can note down her observations using a Referral Form. The form (which can be designed by the teacher to screen those behaviours relevant to the child's academic, social, and emotional background) is a useful method of collecting information about the child. The form can be sent on to the Headmistress who may then call in an expert for further "diagnostic" testing. With older students, the teacher can conduct an informal interview or use a questionnaire.

When making observations, teachers should consider the following guidelines:

1. Be specific about the behaviours observed. A behaviour must be operational in measurable terms, for example, it is not enough

to say "Deepa is not reading well." Instead, "reading" should be quantified as "When reading, Deepa misses words, omits vowel sounds i and e, and cannot recognize sight words." Similarly, instead of observing that a student "is inattentive," it is better to specify exactly under what conditions the student is inattentive. Is it when listening to teacher's instructions? Initiating a class activity? Or, failing to complete a worksheet?

2. Avoid biased observations. This is indeed very difficult because most teachers have automatically judged the child before even the observation has begun. Still it is in the best interests of the child if the teacher tries to be impartial when collecting information about the child.
3. Vary the observations over different periods and settings. When observing children, its always a good idea to vary the time and setting of the observation. For example, a child may perform very poorly just after lunch or before a science class; but do much better in the art room or on the playground.
4. Use a systematic recording procedure. This can be quite time consuming so it is important to be specific about the target behaviour one is observing. Usually teachers prefer to use an event sampling or time sampling procedure. In time sampling, a behaviour is recorded at specific intervals; for example, the teacher records how many times Deepa is "off-task" during a five-minute period. In event sampling, every time Deepa is off-task (talking to others, getting out of her seat etc.), the event is recorded.
5. Observe if the child is using any strategies when approaching a task. For example, did he subtract from left to right? Did he use tally marks? What methods does he use for checking his work? Also observe the time taken to complete the task.

Checklists and Rating Scales are another way of collecting behavioural data. Many behaviour scales are available commercially such as the Behaviour Assessment System for Children, Second edition (BASC-2).

The Role of Professionals in the Assessment Process

Learning-disabled children need the support of a multi-disciplinary team consisting of regular teachers, specialists, psychologists, speech therapists, physicians, and school counselors. A neurologist may also be approached if parents suspect some kind of neurological dysfunction. Generally, the neurologist will collect information pertaining to birth and developmental history, and examine the child's total neurological functioning, sometimes using an EEG (Electroencephalography).

A licensed psychologist should conduct the psychological tests. Parents should not hesitate to ask questions relating to any aspect of their child's assessment. Do not remain content with a static number that defines your child's intelligence. Ask what can be done to improve his learning, what are the areas which he finds difficult, and why learning is *not* taking place. Work with the psychologist as an active participant in the child's future, not as a passive observer of events "happening" to the child. Some commonsense rules can be followed. Ensure your child is tested when he is bright and alert, not sleepy and tired. Some children do not test well on time-bound tests and this factor *must* be considered before damning the child as slow. Prolonged sickness may lead to academic lags, which could also affect performance.

After Diagnosis, What?

After the child is identified as having a specific learning disability, most parents do not know what kind of help to seek; or, how to make the school accountable to the child. What is the role of the schools in helping their child? Can the school provide any special services? What are other possible alternatives to "normal" schooling? Can parents seek legal help if the school insists on retaining their child year after year, despite the fact the child has a confirmed learning disability? Can the school ask the parents to remove the child? These are important questions that need to be asked and answered.

Schools must take greater responsibility for providing support services for learning disabled students. There must be at least one full-time teacher on the staff who is a fully trained "special educator," with professional experience in using specific remedial methods in teaching reading, writing, and mathematics. Probably the most critical role is that played by the class teacher. Ideally, a teacher dealing with a learning disabled student should have some specialized knowledge of the disability or at least be familiar with remedial principles of teaching. It is not enough to draw parents' attention to the fact that "there is something wrong with your child." Rather, teachers should add, "I think I can help your child!" If outside tutoring is needed it is the teacher's responsibility to maintain regular meetings with the tutor. The teacher is the single most important factor in assessment because the first referral usually comes from the teacher who then maintains a continuous "watch" over the child's progress. Unfortunately in India schools are under no legal obligation to provide special services to the learning disabled students, unlike Western countries where referral is compulsorily followed by an evaluation conducted by a multi-disciplinary team. It is this lack of responsiveness from schools that parents find frustrating.

CHAPTER 10

Enabling Children to Learn

Designing a Remedial Program

The process of assessment should lead to the development of an action plan, often described by different names such as a remedial program, an Individual Education Plan (IEP), "literacy support," and so on. In many countries, the school authorities are legally required to write up the teaching plan, share it with parents, and document whether the student is meeting the objectives. In India, no such law exists but it is still helpful to use the practical, explicit components available in an IEP. Teachers should constantly monitor students' progress and keep their teaching strategies flexible. In order to be successful, the remedial program must have the collaboration and support of the school principal, teachers, and other professionals. It involves a great deal of teamwork, planning and cooperation.

Components of an Individualized Educational Plan (IEP)

The IEP should typically contain the following information:

1. A statement of the child's present level of educational performance.
2. A statement of annual goals, and the short-term objectives.
3. The nature of the services the child will receive.
4. Starting and ending dates of services.
5. A statement of criteria for evaluating how successfully the educational goals are being met.

Current Educational Performance

It is important to assess the child's current level of functioning in both academic and nonacademic areas. This information or baseline data establishes a starting point against which the child's later progress can be measured. The information can be collected using the informal assessment procedures described in Chapter 9. In addition, it may be helpful to note other environmental factors that could be hindering the child's learning – large classroom size, interpersonal relationships with teachers, peers and others, and other social-emotional factors.

Annual Goals and Short-Term Objectives

The educational goals should be a statement of what the child is expected to achieve by year-end. The goals should be in order of priority, sequenced according to the set of skills required in each area. Chandler (1980, pp.16–18) suggested the following questions could be used as a guideline when formulating the annual goals:

1. Are chosen goals practical and relevant to the social, academic, and/or vocational needs of the students?
2. Do the goals reflect the priority needs of the student (simple to complex, immediacy of needs, etc.)?
3. Are the goals realistic in terms of the student's current level of representative (typical) performance?

Nature of the Services to be Provided

Ideally, schools should share in the responsibility to provide support services for the learning disabled student. The IEP should mention "who" will provide "what" kind of help to the child. Some students may need occupational therapy, or speech and language therapy. Others may need ongoing instruction from a special educator. The services required will depend on the degree of disability, the presence of other handicapping conditions, and so on.

Duration of Services

It is important for the IEP document to state when the remedial program will start functioning and for how long the child will receive special help. This keeps both teacher and student on target and helps them to work within a realistic time frame.

Evaluation of Progress

Objectives should be periodically reviewed to ensure that the instructional strategies are appropriate to the child's level of functioning. The teacher must know how to assess when the student has attained mastery, and when to set more challenging goals.

From this discussion, it becomes clear that a remedial program needs a systematic, comprehensive approach and input from many professionals. Ultimately however it is the teacher who has to shoulder responsibility for the child's learning. Most teachers feel an individualized education plan requires a great deal of time, energy and resources, and that it is impractical to expect them to concentrate solely on the needs of a single child to the exclusion of the others.

A remedial program can be successful only if school principals, too, realize that implementing it will increase the teachers' burden and that teachers would need assistance and resources.

Schools must take greater responsibility in providing remedial help for learning disabled children. There must be at least one full-time teacher on the staff who is a fully trained "special educator," and has experience with using specific remedial methods in teaching reading, writing, and mathematics. Large classroom size is the most frequently quoted obstacle to good teaching but a bigger drawback is not having teachers with proper training. The philosophy of the Principal also counts for a great deal. Most principals do lip service to education but will not allow a dyslexic reader to use a computer in class! Parents are not permitted to disagree with the management should their child be asked to repeat a year. Retention is a major area of conflict, with schools rigidly refusing to modify their examination procedures.

The National Open School system offers another alternative to learning disabled students. Parents and educators can access the details on the website www.nos.org. The NOS has come as a blessing for many students as it allows them to pace their learning.

Other Program Options

Occasionally, learning disabled students may need more support than can be provided by the school. Figure 10.1 presents other program options typically available for students with a learning disability.

Residential programs for LD students

↓

Special public or private day-school programs for LD students

↓

Full-day specialized LD services in a self-contained program

↓

Placement in regular classes with part-time, specialized services in a resource room program

↓

Placement in full-day regular classes with teacher support provided by teacher consultant

↓

Placement in full-day regular classes with special teaching provided

Figure 10.1: Major Program Options

Resource Room Model

The resource room model is ideally suited to schools in the Indian school system where large classroom size does not permit the teacher to give attention on an individual basis. Children with learning disabilities may need help in one or more of the academic areas (reading, writing, spelling, oral and written comprehension, mathematics). Instruction in these areas can occur in the resource room, which is staffed by a special educator or reading/math specialist. She works in collaboration with the classroom teachers, setting annual and short-term objectives, designing worksheets which can be used in class, monitoring student's progress, meeting parents and so on. The resource room teacher must be a full-time staff member, and experience has shown that recruiting "part-time" experts works out to be inefficient. A key factor in the success of the resource room facility is scheduling the timetable in such a way that the child does not feel he is isolated and yet receives the maximum help possible. For example, Deepak in Class 6 is reading at Class 4 level. The class teacher has complained that Deepak cannot cope with the level of instruction in class and spends most of the period wandering around the room, distracting other students, or drawing pictures in his art book. Deepak would benefit by going to the resource room five times a week during the English class where he could receive individual, specialized instruction.

A word of caution – the resource room model should not become a dumping ground for students who are difficult to manage. On an average, one teacher can generally serve 8 students and it would be self-defeating to increase the numbers in the resource room simply because teachers in the regular classroom cannot manage them.

Coordinating instruction with methods and materials must be viewed as a challenge. A concern voiced by parents and teachers is that removing students during class time would be detrimental both to their self-esteem ("they would feel different") and to their academic and social interactions. However, this has not been demonstrated. Students generally respond wonderfully to the individual attention provided in the small-group instructional settings. They can clarify their difficulties, ask questions confidently and discuss their problems without embarrassment. It also prevents the child from going to tuitions after school, which can be expensive. The resource room model creates accountability *within* the school system for the child's academic progress.

The role of the teacher (both the specialist and the regular classroom teacher) is critical to the success of the student. The teacher has to be willing to modify her teaching methods, and use any creative approaches she can think of. For example, she can use oral testing, replace essay type questions with a multiple-choice format, permit the student to write assignments on the computer, and in some cases, allow a "writer" (such as used by visually impaired students). It takes a good teacher to understand that the dyslexic student is usually under tremendous pressure, and she will avoid comments such as "he doesn't try hard enough," or "she is lazy."

Itinerant Program

In the itinerant model, an expert teacher is appointed to come into school on specific days of the week to teach the children with learning disabilities. This itinerant teacher generally works with several schools. However, one major drawback of this model is that the teacher tends to function in isolation from the other staff members, and the team approach, which is so essential, is difficult to inculcate.

Special Day-School Programs

Removing the child from school and placing him in a specialized "learning disability facility" is an extremely drastic measure and must be used only as a last resort. Even so, nothing can replace the socialization process that children undergo in a school setting. The schooling years are critical for development and parents must carefully weigh the pros and cons before they decide to remove the child from school to an alternative setting. It would of course be much more encouraging if schools were to change *their* attitude and adopt more flexible approaches to students with learning disability. This would go a long way in preventing exploitation of the child by private organizations that claim to provide a "quick-fix" remedy.

Accommodations in the Indian School Curriculum

The Central Board of Secondary Education (CBSE) and the Indian School Certificate Examination (ICSE) permits several accommodations for students with a learning disability. These include:

- Use of the computer
- Provision of extra time

- Use of a calculator/table grid for mathematics
- Least restrictive marking for spelling and punctuation errors
- Exemption from a second language requirement

These accommodations can start at any grade level and continue into high school, and University. Parents can submit an application form to the Board at the beginning of Grade 9 to avail of these accommodations.

Some Principles of Good Teaching

There is no substitute for good teaching. Often teachers are worried and anxious whether having a learning disabled child in their class would take up all their time; or, if the teacher requires specific skills. Let's not forget that some of the best teaching strategies have evolved when teachers have had to face the challenge of teaching special needs children. Here are some general guidelines for good teaching that serve as a timely reminder that what these students need, above everything else, is a teacher with the right attitude.

Do Not Be Biased

Teachers assume that a child will never learn simply because they have been told the child has a learning disability. Instead of making assumptions, read more about the subject, and prepare yourself for better ways to help the student. Don't be afraid to experiment and adopt flexible ways of evaluating and teaching.

Provide Structure

Most learning-disabled students need a highly structured learning environment. This means classroom expectations should be clearly explained. What should the student do when he is unable to understand the teacher's instructions? Whom can he ask for help? Keep aside 10 minutes when he can approach you to review any steps he has not understood. A "homework basket" on the teacher's desk will remind him he has to turn in his homework every morning. A copy of the day's schedule pasted on the desk will visually reinforce the student which books he needs for each class.

Be Flexible

Each learning disabled student has unique learning needs, which the teacher has to meet. This is called differentiated instruction. The teacher has to match the task with the student's interests and learning characteristics. The teacher should be willing to adopt different strategies and learning aides in the class. This could be very difficult in our educational system, which is very rigidly geared to the CBSE examination, rote memorization, and a fixed syllabus. Teachers must not hesitate to experiment with innovative teaching methods.

The Role of the Parents

Parents have a critical role to play in their child's education. Parents can advocate for their child's right to a fair and proper education only when they are well equipped with knowledge and facts so its vital they educate themselves and keep abreast with new literature and research. Making a support group works well as it creates a forum where parents can share ideas. Remember also that your child needs to know he has your unconditional love and support. Parents must give positive messages to their child who may probably be getting a lot of negativity in school. Encourage your child to participate in a hobby or interest where he can shine.

Here are some questions that parents frequently ask, and may like answers to.

Should I Tell My Child He has Dyslexia?

Absolutely. Tell him that the word *Dys* means difficult and *lexia* means words. Putting them together, *dyslexia* means you have difficulty reading and sometimes this can affect writing and numbers. There are many famous people who are dyslexic (choose examples depending on his age and interests), which proves that dyslexia has nothing to do with intelligence.

How Do You Get Dyslexia?

Children are born with dyslexia. It is not a disease or virus but a problem caused from confusing sounds in words.

Can My Child Go to College?

Yes! There is nothing that can stop your child from pursuing his dreams of higher education. He may need support systems in place for the dreams to come true, but there is no need for you to lower your expectations. Treat your child as a human being capable of leading a full life, and not merely as a learned disabled person.

Resources for Parents

Books

Overcoming Dyslexia by Sally Shaywitz.

Colleges for Students With Learning Disabilities or ADD, Manual published by Petersons Publishing.

Beyond Baby Talk: From Sounds to Sentences, A Parent's Complete Guide to Language Development by Kenn Apel & Julie Masterson.

A Mind At A Time by Mel Levine.

I Wish I Could Fly Like a Bird by Katherine Denison.

Meeting the Challenge of Learning Disabilities in Adulthood by Arlyn J. Roffman

Straight Talk About Reading: How Parents Can Make a Difference During the Early Years by Susan Hall & Louisa Moats.

Succeeding with LD: 20 True Stories About Real People with LD by Jill Lauren.

The Differentiated Classroom: Responding to the Needs of All Learners by Carol Ann Tomlinson.

The Writing Dilemma: Understanding Dysgraphia by Regina G. Richards.

Unlocking Potential: College and Other Choices for People With LD and ADHD by Juliana M. Taymans (Editor), Lynda L. West (Editor), Madeline Sullivan (Editor), Barbara Scheiber (Editor).

Websites

www.ldonline.org
www.schwablearning.org
www.kidsource.com
www.learningdisabilities.org.uk

Appendices

Appendix 1

Resources for Reading

Instructional Programs to Teach Phonics/ Phonological Awareness

Reading Mastery (www.sra4kids.com) is a highly structured reading program, for children in grades kindergarten through six.

Ladders to Literacy (Paul Brookes) for kindergarten.

Phonemic awareness in Young Children: A Classroom Curriculum (Paul Brookes) for kindergarten and first grade.

Phonological Awareness Training for Reading (PRO-ED) for kindergarten through second grade)

Road to the Code (Paul Brookes) (www.brookespublishing.com).

Open Court Reading offers systematic, explicit instruction of phonemic awareness, phonics and word knowledge, comprehension skills and strategies, inquiry skills and strategies, and writing and language arts skills and strategies. It can be ordered at www.sra4kids.com.

Read, Write & Type! Learning System (www.readwritetype.com) useful for first graders.

Jolly Phonics (www.jollylearning.co.uk)

Letterland (www.letterland.com).

For Older Students

Language! A Literacy Intervention Curriculum (www.language-usa.net)

READ 180 (www.scholastic.com)

REACH System (www.sra4kids.com)

Instructional Programs to Teach Reading Fluency

Great Leaps Reading (www.greatleaps.com).

ReadIt (www.reading-assistant.com) helps fluency in grades two through five.

Read Naturally www.readnaturally.com

Ultimate Word Attack for students in middle and high school. www.smartkidssoftware.com

Appendix 2

Resources for Written Language

A. Spelling Programs

1. Alpha to Omega (Beve Hornsby & Frula Shear, Heinemann Educational Books). This program uses a "Read, Write and Spell" approach.
2. The Orton-Gillingham program - www.orton-gillingham.com
3. Explode the Code by Nancy Hall. www.explodethecode.com

B. Instructional Materials to Teach Handwriting

1. *Handwriting Without Tears (HWT, 1997) by Richard Wanderman*
   The curriculum uses multi-sensory techniques and consistent habits for letter formation to teach handwriting to all students—Pre-K through Cursive. In addition, HWT provides parents and teachers the instructional techniques and activities to help improve a child's self-confidence, pencil grip, body awareness, posture and so much more! Order from www.hwtears.com
2. The *AlphaSmart* keyboard is a small, lightweight electronic writing tool that can give people many of the benefits of a portable computer without the complexity or expense.
3. *The Magic Ruler* (Revised) by A.J. Kirschner, O.D. This program to remedy reversals is an error-free introduction to reading and writing letters and numerals that are easily reversed for preschool, primary-grade and older elementary students in remedial programs. The "Magic Rulers" make it impossible to write reversible letters and numbers (such as b-d, m-w, 2–5, 6–9, etc.) the wrong way. The revised manual contains a wealth of activities that give children practice in letter writing. The exercise worksheets are reproducible. Additional dictation words, which correspond to the worksheet exercises, have been included. Order from: www.healthyplace.com

More Information on Dysgraphia:

Richards, Regina G. *When Writing's A Problem* RET Center Press. This booklet defines and outlines the stages of writing, the effects of different pencil grips on writing, and dysgraphic symptoms. Guidelines are provided to identify dysgraphic students and specific helps and compensations are provided.

Levine, Melvin. *Educational Care: A System for Understanding and Helping Children with Learning Problems at Home and in School.* Cambridge, MA: Educators Publishing Service, 1994. Concise, well organized descriptions of specific learning tasks, variations in the ways students process information, and concrete techniques that teachers and parents can use to bypass areas of difficulty.

Related Articles

Diagnosis and Intervention Strategies for Disorders of Written Language by Margaret Kay, Ed. D.

Understanding why Students Avoid Writing by Regina Richards (author of several excellent resources for/about dysgraphia)

LD OnLine In Depth: Writing (Many articles about writing and learning disabilities)

Keyboarding programs for students with special needs – part of LD OnLine's listing of Assistive Technology Resources for Students with Learning Disabilities.

Making Technology Work in the Inclusive Classroom: A Spell CHECKing Strategy for Students with Learning Disabilities – 1998 – Dr. Tamarah Ashton, Ph.D. This strategy helps the student with learning disabilities get the most out of spell checking software.

From Illegible to Understandable: How word prediction and speech synthesis can help. (1998). Charlies A. MacArthur. New software helps writers by predicting the word the student wants to type and reading what s/he has written. How, and how much, does this help with student writing and spelling?

APPENDIX 3

Resources for Mathematics

Instructional Materials and Programmes

Mathematics Textbooks, Materials, and Manipulatives By Monica A. Lambert, Florida, Atlantic University.

TouchMath has now become the most accepted and widely used basic math supplement in special education, general classroom and home learning environments throughout the United States and many foreign countries. Available from www.touchmath.com.

Cuisenaire Rods (Cuisenaire Company of America, Inc.) www.etacuisenaire.com

Cuisenaire rods give students an opportunity to explore concretely mathematical concepts. The basic set includes solid plastic or wooden rods of ten different colours. Instruction begins with learning about the rods through unstructured play. Later, direct play opportunities enable guided discovery of the rods' attributes and specific mathematical concepts and relationships. Accompanying instructional guides outline procedures for teaching (1) counting, (2) one-to-one correspondence, (3) spatial relationships, (4) symmetry, (5) addition, (6) subtraction, (7) multiplication, (8) division, (9) fractions, (10) area, (11) math vocabulary, and (12) problem solving.

Number – Blox (Palo Alto, California, Creative Publications)

These are concrete blocks of the base ten system. The accompanying handbook *Basic Ten Activities* contains detailed explanations of how to develop number concepts and skills through manipulative experiences.

Unifix Materials (Palo Alto, California, Creative Publications)

The set provides a concrete means for teaching numeration systems and number relationships. Each cube has an interlocking device and permits rods to be physically connected or separated. A Unimath activities book has lessons and activities for teaching prenumber concepts, operations, measurement, and fractions.

Real Life Math

www.proedinc.com

Here's an alternative method of teaching consumer math. Students learn a wide range of math skills within a context of basic simulation. This format allows students to learn math skills in conjunction with one another rather than in isolation. All students can benefit from learning consumer math; however, for students who struggle in school, this approach might be the only way they will ever really learn needed everyday math skills. Students who have previously failed in math can succeed with this program because it offers an opportunity to learn by doing.

Distar Arithmetic I, II (Chicago: Science Research Associates)

This is a basal arithmetic series for preschool through grade 3. Order from www.sraonline.com.

Figure It Out (Chicago: Follett Publishing Company) www.tki.org.nz

This is a developmental series that presents basic math skills. The materials are appropriate for students with low reading skills.

Mulching Mathematics to Students with Learning Disabilities—Fourth Edition by Nancy S. Bley & Carol A. Thornton.

Appendix 4

An Analysis of Some Common Errors Children Make in Elementary School Mathematics

Analysis	Example
1. Lacks mastery of basic addition combinations	$\begin{array}{r}3\\+4\\\hline 7\end{array}\quad\begin{array}{r}2\\3\\\hline 4\end{array}$ (circled)
2. Lacks mastery of basic subtraction combinations	$\begin{array}{r}3\\-2\\\hline 1\end{array}\quad\begin{array}{r}8\\5\\\hline 2\end{array}$ (circled)
3. Lacks mastery of basic multiplication combinations.	$\begin{array}{r}3\ 2\\\times\ 3\\\hline 86\end{array}$
4. Lacks mastery of basic division combinations.	$35 \div 5 = 6$ $\begin{array}{r}6\\9\overline{)56}\\-56\\\hline 0\end{array}$
5. Subtracts incorrectly within the division algorithm.	$\begin{array}{r}70\\3\overline{)230}\\-21\\\hline 10 \leftarrow\\-9\\\hline 1\end{array}$

Error	Example
6. Error in addition of partial product.	432 ×57 ——— 3 (0) 24 21 (6) 0 24 (0) 24
7. Does not complete addition: (a) Does not write regrouped number. (b) Leaves out numbers in column addition.	85 +43 ——— 28 4 8 2 ← +3 ——— 15
8. Rewrites a numeral without computing.	→ 72 +15 ——— → 77 → 32 × 3 ——— → 36
9. Does not complete subtraction.	582 −35 ——— 47
10. Does not complete division because of incompleted subtraction.	40) 7)397 −280 ——— 7 7
11. Fails to complete division: stops at first partial quotient.	50 7)370 350
12. Fails to complete division: leaves remainder greater than divisor.	80 R 9 9)729 720 ——— 9

13. Does not complete multiplication within division algorithm.	1) 201 R 3 200) 3) 603 600 3
14. Does not add by bridging endings – should think 5 + 9 = 14, so 35 + 9 = 44.	35 +9 33
15. Lacks additive identity concept in addition	35 +20 50
16. Confuses multiplicative identity within addition operation.	71 +13 73
17. Lacks additive identity concept in substraction.	43 –20 20
18. Confuses role of zero in subtraction with role of zero in multiplication.	37 –20 10
19. Subtracts top-digit from bottom digit whenever regrouping is involved with zero is minuend.	30 –18 28
20. Confuses role of zero in multiplication with multiplicative identity.	7 x 0 = 7
21. Confuses place value of quotient by adding extract zero.	20 30)60
22. Omits zero in quotient.	30 R 3 4)1203 1200 3

23. Lacks facility with addition algorithm: (a) Adds ones to ones and tens:	37 +2 — 59
(b) Adds tens to tens and hundreds:	342 +36 — 678
(c) Adds ones to tens and hundreds:	132 +6 — 798
(d) Is unable to add horizontally: Thinks: 3 + 7 + 1 = 11; writes 1 4 + 3 = 7 (+1 carried) 5 = 5 May add zero to make sum greater than largest addend: 1850	345 + 7 + 13 = 185 8 5 — 185
24. Does not regroup ones to tens.	37 +25 — 52
25. Does not regroup tens to hundreds (or hundreds to thousands).	973 +862 — 735
26. Regroups when unnecessary.	43 +24 — 77
27. Writes regrouped tens digit in ones place, carries ones digit (writes the 1 and carries the 2 from "12").	2 35 +7 — 51○
28. When there are fewer digits in subtrahend: (a) subtracts ones from ones and from tens (*and* hundres)	783 −2 — 561
(b) subtracts tens from tens and hundreds.	783 −23 — 560

29. Does not rename tens digit after regrouping.	54 −9 55
30. Does not rename hundreds digit after regrouping.	532 −181 451
31. Does not rename hundreds or tens when renaming ones.	906 −238 778
32. Does not rename tens when zero is in tens place, although hundreds are renamed.	803 −478 335
33. When there are two zeroes in minuend, renames hundreds twice but does not rename tens.	5 6 700 326 248
34. Decreases hundreds digit by one when unnecessary.	3 7 1 − 1 3 4 1 3 7
35. Uses ones place factor as addend.	32 ×4 126
36. Adds regrouped number to tens but does not multiply. *7 x 1 = 4; 30 + 30 = 60	35 ×7 65*
37. Multiplies digits withing one factor: *4 x 1 = 4; 1 x 30 = 30	31 ×4 34*
38. Multiplies by only one number.	457 ×12 914

---

39. "Carries" wrong number.

$$\begin{array}{r} 8 \\ 67 \\ \times 40 \\ \hline 3220 \end{array}$$

---

40. Does not multiply ones times tens.

$$\begin{array}{r} 32 \\ \times 24 \\ \hline 648 \end{array}$$

---

41. Reverses divisor with dividend.
*Thinks 6 ÷ 3 instead of 30 ÷ 6

$$\begin{array}{r} 2^{*} \\ 6\overline{)30} \end{array}$$

---

42. Does not regroup; treats each column as separate addition example.

$$\begin{array}{r} 23 \\ +\ 8 \\ \hline 211 \end{array}$$

---

43. Subtracts smaller digit from larger at all times to avoid renaming.

$$\begin{array}{r} 273 \\ -639 \\ \hline 446 \end{array}$$

---

44. Does not add regrouped number.

$$\begin{array}{r} 37 \\ \times\ 7 \\ \hline 219 \end{array}$$

---

45. Confuses place value in division:

(a) Considers thousands divided by ones as hundreds divided by ones:

$$\begin{array}{r} 1) \\ 200) \\ 3\overline{)6003} \\ \underline{6000} \\ 3 \\ 3 \end{array}$$

(b) Records partial quotient as tens instead of ones:

$$\begin{array}{rl} 50) & \\ 100) & 150 \\ 7\overline{)735} & \\ \underline{700} & \\ 35 & \\ \underline{35} & \end{array}$$

(c) Omits zero needed to show no ones in quotient.

$$\begin{array}{rl} 2 & \\ 7\overline{)61} & \text{R } 1 \\ \underline{6} & \\ 1 & \end{array}$$

---

46. Ignores remainder because:
    (a) does not complete subtraction;
    (b) does not see need for further computation;
    (c) does not know what to do with "2" if subtraction occurs, so does not compute further.

$$\begin{array}{r} 80 \\ 7\overline{)562} \\ \underline{560} \\ 2 \end{array}$$

Source: F.K. Reisman. *A Guide to the Diagnostic Teaching of Arithmetic* (3rd.ed.) Columbus. Ohio Charles E. Merrill Publishing Company, 1982 pp.130–36. Reprinted with permission of the publisher)

APPENDIX 5

Resources for Adult Dyslexics

Reading Resources

Language!

The program is systematically laid out with each unit of study rated according to level of reading difficulty. The reader can access thousands of books, drawn from different genres. Order from www.sopriswest.com

The Wilson Learning System uses manipulatives to teach phonics and word analysis skills. It stresses fluency and spelling. Materials are motivating and inetersting for adults. The program is completed in 3–4 years.

Starting Over (www.epsbooks.com) is a supplemtnal program for adults already attending in an adult literacy class.

Lexia Reading SOS (strategies for Older Students) is a software reading program that can be used as a supplemental reading program. It can be ordered from www.lexialearning.com

Accommodations for Students with LD

By: National Center for Learning Disabilities (2006)

What are Accommodations?

Accommodations are alterations in the way tasks are presented that allow children with learning disabilities to complete the same assignments as other students. Accommodations do not alter the content of assignments, give students an unfair advantage or in the case of assessments, change what a test measures. They do make it possible for students with LD to show what they know without being impeded by their disability.

How Does a Child Receive Accommodations?

Once a child has been formally identified with a learning disability, the child or parent may request accommodations for that child's specific needs. The Individuals with Disabilities Education Act states that a child's IEP (Individualized Education Program) team which both parent and child are a part of must decide which accommodations are appropriate for him or her. Any appropriate accommodations should be written into a student's IEP.

Here are some examples of possible accommodations for an IEP team to consider, broken into six categories:

- Presentation:
    - Provide as a recording
    - Provide in large print
    - Reduce number of items per page or line
    - Provide a designated reader
    - Present instructions orally
- Response:
    - Allow for verbal responses
    - Allow for answers to be dictated to a scribe
    - Allow the use of a recorder to capture responses
    - Permit responses to be given via computer
    - Permit answers to be recorded directly into test booklet
- Timing:
    - Allow frequent breaks
    - Extend allotted time for a test
- Setting:
    - Provide preferential seating
    - Provide special lighting or acoustics
    - Provide a space with minimal distractions
    - Administer a test in small group setting
    - Administer a test in private room or alternative test site

- Test Scheduling
  - Administer a test in several timed sessions or over several days
  - Allow subtests to be taken in a different order
  - Administer a test at a specific time of day
- Other
  - Provide special test preparation
  - Provide on-task/focusing prompts
  - Provide any reasonable accommodation that a student needs that does not fit under the existing categories

Should Accommodations Have an Impact on How Assignments are Graded?

School assignments and tests completed with accommodations should be graded the same way as those completed without accommodations. After all, accommodations are meant to "level the playing field," provide equal and ready access to the task at hand, and not meant to provide an undue advantage to the user.

What If Accommodations Don't Seem to be Helping?

Selecting and monitoring the effectiveness of accommodations should be an ongoing process, and changes (with involvement of students, parents and educators) should be made as often as needed. The key is to be sure that chosen accommodations address students' specific areas of need and facilitate the demonstration of skill and knowledge.

The Central Board of Secondary Education (CBSE) has issued rules for providing accommodations to students with varying special needs. Learning disability is included in this category. Refer to https://www.cbse.gov.in/cbsenew/Examination_Circular/2018/3_CIRCULAR.pdf